THE ART OF MINIMALISM

A SIMPLE GUIDE TO DECLUTTER AND ORGANIZE YOUR LIFE

Olivia Telford

THE ART OF MINIMALISM:
A Simple Guide to Declutter and Organize Your Life
by Olivia Telford

© **Copyright 2019 by Olivia Telford**

All Rights Reserved.

ISBN-10: 1687418209
ISBN-13: 978-1687418203

ALSO BY OLIVIA TELFORD

*Hygge: Discovering The Danish Art Of Happiness –
How To Live Cozily And Enjoy Life's Simple Pleasures*

*Mindfulness: The Remarkable Truth Behind Meditation
and Being Present in Your Life*

*Cognitive Behavioral Therapy: Simple Techniques to Instantly
Overcome Depression, Relieve Anxiety, and Rewire Your Brain*

CONTENTS

INTRODUCTION

Greetings readers! First, I want to thank you for purchasing my book, as it has always been my lifelong passion to help others. In my moments of despair, when I didn't think there was any hope, I couldn't even fathom the idea of one day being able to turn my mess into a message. However, with much determination, study, and application of what I have learned, and experiencing a dramatic transformation in my life, I am now able to pass on what I have learned and help others live a better life by becoming the best version of themselves. Second, I want to congratulate you for taking the bold step towards change, because I can tell you from my own personal experience that it is not easy.

We live in a world that tells us that in order to be happy we must acquire more goods. Everywhere we look and everywhere we turn we are bombarded with images of what it means to be prosperous and successful, but what ends up happening is that we become overwhelmed with the meaningless goods we have acquired. Clutter in the home creates disorder, and disorder in the home creates chaos in our lives.

In this book you will learn that there is much more to clutter than you thought. Not only am I going to teach you how to eliminate clutter from your home, but also how to eliminate clutter from your relationships, emotions, and much more, so that you can live the happy and prosperous life that you know you deserve!

In order to maximize the value you receive from this book, I highly encourage you to join our tight-knit community on Facebook. Here you will be able to connect and share with other like-minded Minimalists to continue your growth.

Taking this journey alone is not recommended, and this can be an excellent network for you.

It would be great to connect with you there,

Olivia Telford

To Join, Visit:

www.pristinepublish.com/mindfulgroup

WHAT OTHERS ARE SAYING ABOUT THE ART OF MINIMALISM

"Olivia Telford's The Art of Minimalism shares an invaluable lesson about redesigning your life top to bottom. She redirects you from seeking happiness in consumerism and points you towards relationships, experiences, and soul care –places that you will find life and true lasting happiness. It has made me realize how all the stuff I own has been holding me back from pursuing my dreams. A truly wonderful book that can change your life and keep you organized for years to come."

— Daniel Walter, author of 10-Minute Focus: 25 Habits for Mastering Your Concentration and Eliminating Distractions

"This is an incredible book that shows you how powerful it is to live with less. Highly recommend."

— Bella Jean, author of The Forever In Between: A Historical Western Romance Book

"If you are looking to declutter and experience the joys of peace, contentment and purposeful living than this is the book for you. In The Art of Minimalism you will find comprehensive and straightforward techniques you can use today to instantly improve your home and wellbeing. After reading this book, I've never felt more organized, stress free and productive. Whether you've tried minimalism before or are brand new to it, this is the perfect guide."

— Judy Dyer, author of Empath: A Complete Guide for Developing Your Gift and Finding Your Sense of Self

DOWNLOAD THE AUDIO VERSION OF THIS BOOK FREE

If you love listening to audiobooks on-the-go or would enjoy a narration as you read along, I have great news for you. You can download the audio book version of *The Art of Minimalism* for FREE (Regularly $6.95) just by signing up for a FREE 30-day audible trial!

Visit: www.pristinepublish.com/audiobooks

YOUR FREE GIFT - 10 MINUTE MEDITATION

'm sorry to be the bearer of bad news, but life isn't about you! And the moment you accept this is when you will truly start living. We live in a world that justifies selfishness, and everything is about the self. The dominant thought process goes, "What am I going to get out of this? How is this situation going to benefit me? Who can I manipulate to give me what I want?" Society has trained us to believe that the more money we have, the more we can buy, and the happier we will be. But the evidence suggests that these things don't bring us fulfilment. Why? Because the ego is always going to want more. Some of the most successful people in the world are never satisfied. The private jet is never enough, multiple partners are never enough, a wardrobe full of designer clothes is never enough. The 25-room mansion, and properties all over the world are never enough. If the world has got it wrong, then what brings true contentment in life?

Knowing that your purpose on earth is to be a giver. We were created to be givers, to empty ourselves using our gifts and talents in order to make the world a better place. Our peace comes from living selflessly, and not selfishly. I believe that the root cause of the human condition is that we are not living the way we were created to live. We've been corrupted and it's causing us to malfunction. The physical manifestation of this is seen through anxiety, depression, stress, and the plethora of mental health issues that we suffer from. Have you noticed that the happiest people are those who have found their purpose, and that purpose is always connected to giving of themselves? That's because they are doing what they were created to do.

"This all sounds great," I hear you saying, "but what do I need to do to get to this point? How can I live a selfless life when I'm struggling with anxiety, overthinking, stress, and depression? I can barely make it through the day, let alone think about living for other people." May I submit to you that meditation is the key to freeing yourself from the mental prison you are currently locked in? Here's how.

Meditation helps you connect with your higher self. Right now, you are living far below your capabilities, but you are more powerful than you could ever imagine. Science proves that meditation rewires the brain. It strengthens certain areas in the brain and transforms your internal emotional state. It makes you more compassionate and improves your ability to focus. Why is that important? Because a wandering mind can't focus on the needs of others. Additionally, several studies have found that meditation is linked to compassionate behavior towards oneself and others. It basically makes us more altruistic, which is exactly what we need if we are going to live to our full potential.

Meditation will teach you how to disconnect from the world so you can connect with your inner world. How much time do you spend on social media connecting meaningfully with people you know? We know more about the lives of the latest celebrities than we do about ourselves. Some people have become so co-dependent that spending time alone scares them. Being continuously engaged has become the norm, and those who enjoy solitude are often ridiculed. But the irony is that solitude is the only way you can truly get to know yourself. Switching off the TV and putting down the phone to tune in to yourself is a terrifying prospect for some of us.

You're not alone. When I first started meditating, I was afraid of getting to know myself too. I was petrified of listening to the voices in my head because I'd spent most of my life running from them. The more I ran, the more I suffered, because I was running into the same like-minded people who didn't like themselves very much either. True love starts from within. If you don't love yourself, it's impossible to love anyone else. And how can you love yourself if you don't know yourself? It took me a while to get to know and love myself, and I'm still learning who I am. When I embraced solitude, and finally surrendered, I really started enjoying my own company. You've just got to take that leap of faith and do it because it works. I now have the peace and freedom I've always wanted. Meditation was a complete game changer for me; it even gave me the confidence to quit my job and start writing full time!

Unfortunately, meditation intimidates many people, and they have no idea how transformative it is. If you were to ask the average person what comes to mind when they think about meditation, they'll say something like, "A monk sitting on top of a hill thinking about nothing for hours." As you will discover, meditation is much more than the stereotypes portray. Furthermore, you can experience the full benefits by meditating for as little as ten minutes each day.

Do you want to enrich your life, free yourself from the burdens of anxiety, stress, and overthinking? Do you want to transcend the human mind and connect with the infinite source? Do you want to live an abundant life overflowing with peace, joy, and happiness? Do you want to find fulfilment in everything you do? Do you want to develop deeper relationships with your loved ones and improve your health? The information in this guide will help you achieve it. In this bonus e-book, you can expect to learn about the following:

- Exactly what meditation is and what it isn't
- The basics of meditation and the different types
- The health benefits of meditation
- Meditation techniques to help you overcome anxiety, stress, overthinking and insomnia

The aim of *10 Minute Meditation* is to take the fear out of meditation and make it accessible to all who desire to improve their lives on a deeper level. I truly believe that what you are about to read will radically transform your life.

Get *10 Minute Meditation* for Free by Visiting

www.pristinepublish.com/meditationbonus

CHAPTER 1:

START BY MAKING YOUR BED

I can already hear you…"Start by making your bed?!" It sounds absolutely ridiculous, doesn't it? But did you know that this is the first lesson that the people who protect your country learn when they enter the military? It sounds completely backward—there is a global crisis of terrorism but bed making is a priority! No matter what country you are in, before the military trains their soldiers to fight on the battlefield, they train them how to make their beds. And I mean rigorous training. If there is ever such thing as a bed making competition, a soldier will win it every time. Why are they trained to make their beds with proper forty-five-degree hospital corners? Is the opposition going to be impressed by their ability to bounce a quarter off the bed? No! The purpose is to instill a habit of excellence into the soldiers. Human beings are creatures of habit—if a person thinks it's okay to leave trash in his car, he will leave it in any car he sits in because that's just what he does. The bottom line is that it's the smallest habits that count. They determine how you are going to do everything else in life. In other words, if a soldier can't make his bed, he has no business defending his country.

Imagine walking into the barracks of the American Army and seeing a line of unmade beds, clothes all over the floor, and the place just looking like an overall hot mess. How much faith would you have in the military? None, right? Your first thought would be, if they can't keep their own living space clean, how can they safeguard the country? If you can't be bothered to make your bed, you won't be bothered when it comes to loading your rifle. A cluttered environment is a reflection of a cluttered mind. I generally find it pretty easy to judge where a person is mentally when I walk into their house. This is why there is so much importance placed on attention to detail in every area of a soldier's training. In the military, beds are called racks, and making a rack in a specific way is not just for cleanliness, but also to ensure that all the soldiers are on the same page.

Navy Seal Admiral Bill McRaven gave a speech at the University of Texas where he spoke about the 10 lessons he learned while he was being trained as a SEAL. It sounded awfully strange to hear such a strong and accomplished man state that he got to where he is today because of something as simple as making his bed! He went on to state that making your bed in the morning is an accomplishment—it gives you a sense of pride that you have achieved something for that day. It also provides momentum and additional encouragement to move onto completing other tasks. Keeping your house in order is not the only thing that's important here; the standards you set for yourself and how much respect you have for yourself and your family is made clear by your environment.

It is also important to note that this is not about pursuing perfection but excellence. People who do things in a spirit of excellence, do mundane, ordinary everyday tasks in an extraordinary way.

The first directive I am giving you in your journey to personal growth is to clean yourself up! I know, this doesn't sound very exciting and it's certainly not the stuff that movies are made of. In fact, it probably sounds pretty foolish if you are someone who's got big dreams, but it's important. The idea here is that if you are faithful with the small things, you will be faithful with the big things. And if you are dishonest with the small things, you will be dishonest with the big things. If you can't get your house in order, how can you get anything else in your life in order? If you want to get anywhere in life, you must adopt a standard of excellence—this is how you prepare for success.

Remember, the way you keep your house is the way you will keep everything else in your life. The standard of excellence you keep is all about preparing yourself for greatness; where you go next in your life is always connected to what you are doing now. Excellence is the key that opens doors of opportunities that will plant your feet on the path to success.

It's interesting how we can become immune to clutter, acclimated to debris, and adjusted to junk. We become so complacent around things that once got on our nerves to no end, that we eventually end up ignoring it as if the clutter is no longer visible. Close your eyes and imagine that you want to sell your house, so you put it on the market in the state that it's in today. Who do you think is going to buy it? No one! It will stay on the market until you clean it up.

There are no short cuts in life—whatever you want is going to take a lot of work, because all great things take time. The question is, are you prepared to put the effort in? Not only to get there but to maintain it. You see, the universe has to know that it can trust you before it gives you what you want. So, if you are only going to keep up your standard of excellence for one month and then slip back into your old habits, don't expect to move forward in life. You will stay stuck in the same old rut until excellence becomes a normal part of your life. The problem is that the majority of people are impatient—the woman who wants a body like Jennifer Lopez can't expect to work out for a few hours and hope to see results. It doesn't work like that, and when people don't see immediate results, they revert back to old habits. Maybe you are like this yourself, or you have a friend like it—for the past two years they have gone on every diet under the sun, but they are still overweight. That's because they never stick to anything long enough to see results.

A lot of people believe that there is no point in making your bed in the morning because you are only going to get back into it at night. May I submit to you that every time you make your bed in the morning you are preparing for greatness.

Most people don't see the point of washing the dishes before they go to bed; after all, they are only going to use more dishes in the morning. May I submit to you that every time you wash the dishes before you go to bed, you are preparing for greatness.

Most people don't see the point in hanging their clothes up when they take them off because they are only going to wear them again the next day. May I submit to you that every time you hang your clothes up in the evening, you are preparing for greatness.

There is a possibility that, like a petulant teenager, you believe that these things are irrelevant, but let me remind you again that it's these small habits and personal standards of excellence that will determine how well you do everything else in life.

CHAPTER 2:

WHAT EXACTLY IS DECLUTTERING?

There is nothing complicated about decluttering. It is a simple process that involves getting rid of the things in your house that you don't need. However, the funny thing is that there are many people who have no idea what decluttering is—their idea of a clear-out is moving things around and making them look neat. That, my friend, is not decluttering! Neither is it buying a new wardrobe, shelves, or drawers and stacking away the things you don't want, and neither is it organizing or filing. You see, when you've shifted things around, organized, or hidden all of your unused items, they are still there taking up unnecessary space, just in a different way. When it comes to decluttering, your focus should be on one thing, and that is getting what you don't need out of the house.

When you do this, not only will you feel as if a weight has been lifted off your shoulders, you will feel that a weight has also been lifted off your home. You will find that your life is much easier, and your home will function much better. Think about it like this, anything in your home that you feel you have no control over is considered clutter. Once you have completed the decluttering process, that should be the yardstick you use to judge whether you are accumulating too many things again.

May I warn you that this process is not going to be easy; in fact, it is very overwhelming, which is why a lot of people choose to rearrange things instead of getting rid of them—it eliminates the decision-making process. However, the best way to overcome this is just to get on with it. Just don't dive right in at the deep end—start with the small things first. For example, a drawer in your bedroom or office, just open it and start throwing out the things you don't need. Once you have made some space and you realize how much better it looks, and how much better it makes you feel, you will be inspired to continue.

It's Not the Size of Your Home—It's You!

I believe that many people move from their home unnecessarily because of all the stuff they've accumulated over the years—their house starts to look like a thrift store. The next thing you know, they are moving into a bigger house, one with more storage space and more rooms; but guess what happens? They pack the house with more things they don't need, and the house ends up looking no different than the one they've just moved out of. Once you finally stop using the spaces you should be the most comfortable in to store the things you don't really need, you will be much happier. In fact, you will start finding rooms and spaces in your home that you didn't know existed! Almost like magic, your house will become bigger than you thought it was.

STOP PUTTING YOUR STUFF BEFORE YOUR SPACE

What's your favorite comfort food? (Please bear with me a moment, I'm going somewhere with this!) Well, mine is whipped vanilla ice cream (the type you got when you were a kid from the ice-cream van) with strawberry juice, nuts, and 2 chocolate flakes poked into the top! The thought of it makes my mouth water! But when I'm stuck in a rut, depressed, or stressed out, I go and find the ice cream man and get me some ice cream. My point is that even though comfort food tastes delicious, it's typically bad for you, and we would all be much better off if we turned to fruit and vegetables for comfort food instead, but hey—wishful thinking right!

My point is that clutter is "comfort food" for some people. Think about the last time you ate some comfort food—it felt really good while you were eating it right? But afterward, you didn't feel so great. Not only because the food was finished but because you knew you were going to put on some extra pounds, and those jeans you just bought would no longer fit. So, when you go to wear those skinny jeans and realize they don't fit, you get frustrated, and that frustration makes you want to eat more comfort foods, so now you've gotten yourself into a vicious cycle that's difficult to break.

This is the same process that takes place when you are constantly buying things that you think you might need in the future. You walk through the store aisles grabbing things because you think they might be of some benefit to you or one of your family members somewhere down the line. However, two years pass, the things have collected an avalanche of dust, but you are still confident that you will use it one day. When you purchased the item, it felt great; but then when you try to clean and have no space, you start complaining that it's so difficult to clean your home! So just as the ice cream turns into frustration when the buttons start to pop, that pleasurable feeling of buying something turns into frustration when you find it difficult to clean or can't find the things you do need because the house is so full of things you don't need! Do you see the connection here?

You start looking at your pile of unnecessary items as even more valuable than the space that you need, simply because you have convinced yourself that you might need them one day. And like your comfort food, this is not healthy. Once you start going through your piles of stuff, you will realize that for every ten items that you don't need, there is only one item that you do need. Once you start getting rid of worthless things, you will find a new love, and that love is space!

WHERE DID ALL THIS STUFF COME FROM ANYWAY?

Once upon a time it was in our best interest to hoard things, resources were scarce, and you didn't know if you'd ever be able to get it again if you threw it out. After the Industrial Revolution, things started to change. You could easily get your hands on a variety of goods and they were relatively cheap. The brainiacs of the world began to invent things such as washing machines, dishwashers, and cars. Life was sweet, and people really didn't need anything else since they had so much leisure time to enjoy. This was when sales started to decline.

Moving onto World War II, the economy had changed and bumped heads with consumer contentment. So, the brainiacs put their heads together again to come up with a strategy to get people buying again, and we transitioned from being content with our dishwashers, washing machines, and cars to over-consumers and buying things that quite frankly, we don't need. What happened? The answer lies in the multi-billion-dollar advertising industry.

Today, it is impossible to walk past an empty store, people are always buying something new. Why? Because marketing companies hire geniuses to create enticing advertising campaigns to convince us to buy what we don't need. Not only that, but they are also using a clever technique called neuromarketing. Advertising companies employ neuroscientists to help them tap into the subconscious mind and shut down the area in the brain responsible for telling us that we don't need something. Instead, advertisements trigger the part of the brain that makes us feel that we are lacking something. Once we are in a state of vulnerability, we are presented with the thing that will fill the void and solve the problem. Are you single? That's probably because you don't have the right clothes to attract the right partner. But if you buy this $150 pair of jeans, you will have all the hot girls swarming around you like bees on honey.

Living a minimalist life requires that you take a break from impulse buying. It means that you are no longer a slave to advertising campaigns and that you have full control over your buying habits. The media is constantly sending us messages that we need more—you have to upgrade your phone, increase your credit limit, buy a newer model car, improve your wardrobe, and the list goes on! These messages are drilled into us and affirmed on every corner—children hear it at school and adults hear it at work. We hear it so much that we believe it, that's why kids cry and stamp their feet until they get the latest toy, and parents go into debt to keep up with the Joneses. But the fact is that you don't need any of these things, and you will realize this once you start living a minimalist life.

Imagine if these messages were reversed, and all we heard was, "Save 80 percent of your income so that you can retire at 40." People would start to believe it and take action towards it. But this message would never become mainstream because it doesn't benefit the bigwigs. They need us to spend our money and get into debt to keep their pockets fat.

CLUTTER IS A WASTE OF TIME, ENERGY, AND SPACE

What happens when you can't find something? No matter what it is, you are going to spend time and energy trying to find it. When your home is overflowing with things you don't use, you are taking up unnecessary space. A messy home can also make you feel frustrated, embarrassed, and anxious. Frustrated because you can never find anything, embarrassed because you see the looks on your friends' faces when they come to your house, and anxious because you are always worried that someone might ring the door at any moment.

You can change this way of living if you really want to. It's going to take time, dedication, and energy, but it will all be well spent. Have you ever stayed in a nice hotel? Do you remember that peaceful feeling when you first walked in? If not, Google one—just looking at how organized the room is gives you a sense of calm and well-being. When you stay in a hotel, you've got just about enough of everything to get you through your stay—one towel, one bar of soap, one book to read, and a few clothes. Life is easy because you don't have to deal with the stress of being surrounded by a bunch of possessions you don't need. What if you could transform the vacation version of you into the real you? The good news is that you can, and there's no time like the present.

Most people don't like tidying up, especially when it's a mammoth task. So, they keep putting it off until next weekend turns into next year! There is more to procrastination than meets the eye. At its core, it's rooted in fear. And when it comes to decluttering, there are certain possessions that can bring dormant emotions to the surface that we really don't want to deal with. In some cases, we have piled a month's worth of laundry on top of our emotions hoping to keep them buried.

Where you live is a reflection of who you are on the inside. When you declutter your home, you have to face parts of yourself that you were trying to ignore. So, to a certain extent, you need to prepare yourself for the emotional upheaval that is about to take place. If possessions were just possessions, getting rid of them wouldn't matter. But in some cases, they come with a whole heap of emotional baggage. But as Lao Tzu says, a journey of a thousand miles starts with one step, and once you take that first step, you will build momentum and start feeling a sense of freedom as you are released from your past.

Now, if you don't have a notebook, I want you to go out and buy one. Not just any old random notebook, a nice one. It might be in your favorite color or have a motivational quote on it, but you will know when you see it. It should be small enough for you to comfortably carry around with you. This will be your decluttering journal and you are going to use it to record your decluttering process—write down how you felt when you threw certain items away, how many bags you have donated to charity. How you felt when you finished your first room, then your second, how you felt after giving yourself that much-deserved reward, etc.

Studies have revealed that no matter how many toys children have, they end up playing with the same toy because they have too many to choose from and it confuses them. Well, children are not the only ones who have too many things, adults do too, and these unnecessary possessions are taking up too much energy, thought, space, and not to mention a waste of money, especially when none of them are providing any real benefit.

Sometimes it feels as if the items in our cupboards, on our shelves, garages, and lofts multiply as soon as we turn our backs! One day, you just look at everything and wonder where it all came from.

Do you have so many things in your kitchen that you struggle to find the space to cook? What about the bathroom? Do you have to move things off the toilet seat when you need to use it? Is your wardrobe about to fall apart because it's so full?

How Do We Accumulate So Much Clutter?

Where does all this stuff come from anyway? Car boot sales, markets, Christmas presents we don't like, souvenirs, eBay, Amazon, Gumtree, and the list goes on. Most of what we now consider clutter doesn't start off that way—clutter is what it turns into when we stop using the items. Yes, there are some things we purchase that we only use once and toss to the side. But we do get some good usage out of the majority of things. So, a part of the problem is that we have a bad habit of buying things we don't really need, and the other half is that we don't know how to throw the things away that we no longer use. These things build up over the years, and when we realize we are running out of space, instead of giving things away or selling them, we buy storage boxes and stuff them in the bottom of wardrobes, in garages, and lofts.

WHY DO WE BUY MORE THAN WE NEED?

There are many reasons why we have developed a habit of buying more than we need.

Souvenirs: We go on vacation or to a town in our country we have never visited before and buy something small and cheap to remind us that we have been there.

Just in Case: Then there are moments when we know we don't need the item now, but we think we will use it later, so we buy it anyway. The problem is that we never end up using it.

We Think We Need It: We are often guilty of believing we need certain things when, in reality, we don't. Like the oven cleaner you just saw advertised on TV, but you already have one and just think that this one being advertised will give your oven an additional shine.

Self-Improvement: We have been conditioned to believe that the more we accumulate the better our lives will be. Or the better we will look.

A BIT OF HISTORY

Before World War II, most kitchens were clutter-free and cooking was done on a stove top or in the oven using a limited amount of pots and pans. The most popular kitchen item before WWII was the cast iron skillet, which could be used on the stove or placed in the oven. They were nonstick and were often inherited from parents or grandparents, meaning that they were very durable.

There was a huge leap in technological advancement after WWII and kitchen gadgets were among the many developments. The microwave oven was discovered by Percy Spencer. As the story goes, he actually discovered it by accident. Spencer was employed by a company called Raytheon who developed microwave transmitters. One day, he left a candy bar in his pocket while he was working on some equipment, and he noticed that it started melting. He decided to start experimenting with the equipment and discovered that microwaves could heat food. Spencer went on to invent the first microwave oven, and the first thing he cooked in it was popcorn.

There is no denying the fact that the microwave was a great invention, but there is also no denying the fact that they take up space in the kitchen! The economic boom gave more people access to products such as refrigerators and freezers, which were only available to the wealthy before the war.

Technology continued to advance, and other equipment such as toasters, rice cookers, pressure cookers, and portable grills were now on the market. All of which took up space on kitchen work surfaces. Today we have pressure cookers that are controlled by smartphone apps!

The post-war period also led to a dramatic shift in our eating habits. More women had entered the workforce, and they had less time to cook. It was during this time that ready-made processed foods became popular. All of which are high in sugar, saturated fats, and carbohydrates. Many experts claim that there was also a steep increase in obesity during this time.

It appears that clutter is a modern-day issue, and more often than not you will hear grandparents complaining about the number of things we have in the home today. Think about it, if people didn't need all this stuff back then, why do we need it now?

CHAPTER 3:

GETTING ORGANIZED – THE BENEFITS

Clutter, mess, junk… whatever you want to call it, when you have no room it causes chaos. It's not just an eyesore, it's bad for your mental and physical well-being. A study conducted by the University of New Mexico discovered that family members felt uncomfortable in a cluttered home. Participants stated that they didn't feel as if it was a home and neither did they feel safe and secure. This relates to the psychologist Abraham Maslow's hierarchy of needs. He presents the basic human needs in pyramid form—our survival needs are at the base of the pyramid, all humans need adequate shelter, sleep, food, water, and homeostasis. He places financial stability and personal safety above this. Next is our need for love and acceptance within a group. At the top of the pyramid is what Maslow refers to as self-actualization, which means that you have fulfilled your potential and have become everything you were destined to be. However, before we arrive here, we must have fulfilled the desires at the bottom of the pyramid.

The home is what we would consider shelter; it is the place where we should feel safe and secure. Clutter makes it impossible to feel secure and therefore, there is a negative psychological impact associated with living in a messy house.

Studies have also found that a messy home is linked to bad eating habits. Think about it, who wants to cook in a kitchen with dishes stacked to the ceiling and trash everywhere? Getting takeout or snacking makes things easier when the kitchen is a mess. Bad eating habits then contribute to bad health, and the vicious cycle begins.

Studies have also found that a cluttered work environment has a negative effect on employee productivity. Clutter makes it difficult for employees to focus, slows down visual processing, and they are easily distracted because there is always something else to focus on other than their work. The brain finds it difficult to differentiate between relevant and irrelevant stimuli, and clutter is considered irrelevant stimuli, causing mental processing to slow down. The old saying that a cluttered house makes a cluttered mind is a proven scientific fact.

Dust and mold build up amongst clutter. When you have too many items in one area, cleaning becomes extremely difficult and it's easy to miss spots and overlook areas. A buildup of dust and mold can cause respiratory problems such as asthma and bronchitis.

Imagine there are two different offices. The first is stacked with books, paperwork, documents, and stationery. There is no room on any of the shelves, and you open a drawer that is crammed full of so much stuff you could hold a garage sale. No doubt there are plenty of interesting books to read and some nice pieces of stationary to work with, but the question is, can you find them when you need to? And if you really do need to look for them, how much time is it going to take? And how do you feel when you think you've found the book you were looking for, but as you go to grab it, the stack of papers resting on the books falls on your head? Or how do you feel when you know you left that luxury pen on the end of the desk but after moving a few items out of the way, you can't seem to find it?

Now, I want you to think about another office. When you walk in there is plenty of space for you to move around. Sure, the shelves have books on them, but they are organized like a library and there are only a few on each shelf. All the paperwork is in folders stored in filing cabinets, and all the stationary is neatly organized in pots and racks. Both offices are exactly the same size, have the same size desks, and the same number of shelves. The only difference between them is the number of items inside the office. The exact same office that just appears completely hopeless and unmanageable can be made to look simple and organized just by getting rid of some of the items. You will find that organization is possible when you throw away what you don't need.

According to the *United States News and World Report*, the average American spends approximately 12 months within the span of their life looking for lost items. Now just think about what you could do with an additional year added to your life. Think about how many extra things you could get done, the business you want to start, the weight you want to lose, the book you want to write, the degree you want to get, or the countries you want to travel to. Instead, you spend an entire year, looking for your keys! How ridiculous does that sound?

Research has discovered that the average home in the United States contains 300,000 items! In saying that, we don't use 80% of what we own! I am trying to get you to understand that the little bit of time you waste every day looking for those items because you have so much clutter and are so disorganized can quickly add up and cause you to miss some major opportunities.

According to the National Association of Professional Organizers, we receive an estimated 49,060 pieces of mail in a lifetime and almost half of it is junk mail. Every year, 16.6 billion catalogs are delivered to 100 million households. These catalogs are then stacked in a pile and left to collect dust, so they simply become more items adding to the clutter in your home.

Research also suggests that getting organized is on the list of top five New Year's resolutions, but only 20% of people get around to actually doing it. So if the majority of people have clutter in their homes, what's the point in me being any different? Here's why:

YOU WILL STOP LOSING THINGS

When was the last time you lost your cell phone or keys? On average, we spend approximately six minutes per day looking for our car keys in the morning. The top five items men are continuously looking for in their homes are the remote control, clean socks, the wedding album, driver's license, and car keys. This list is slightly different for women, which includes lipstick, the remote control, shoes, a child's toy, and wallet.

When your home is tidy and well organized, each item will have its own special place, and when you need it, you will know where to look for it. You will go directly to the filing cabinet for your insurance documents, the key hook on the walls for your car keys, the closet for your jacket, or the top shelf for the remote control. When everything is in order and in its rightful place, you will feel an overwhelming sense of peace.

YOU WILL SAVE MONEY

When was the last time you lost something, went out and bought it only to find the thing that you thought you had lost? Glue, batteries, socks, pens, light bulbs, etc. When your house is organized, you will know exactly where everything is, and you won't need to keep buying things you already own. According to the *Wall Street Journal*, a business adds 20% to their annual budgeting costs when they duplicate or purchase last-minute items. You waste a significant amount of money each time you run to the store to buy batteries that are probably stuck in the bottom of a drawer somewhere. By getting organized, you might even find yourself some lost coupons and save yourself even more money. People also waste money when they can't find their bills and end up paying them late. Statistics show that 23% of adults end up paying late fees, not because they couldn't afford to pay the bill but because they lost the bill!

Disorganization burns holes in your pockets. When you are clutter-free and organized, you won't need to rent a storage facility to house all the belongings that you don't actually need because you won't have any excess items to store! The clever people are making money out of your disorganization—storage facilities have become a $154 billion industry. Statistics state that one in eleven Americans at any one time are renting a unit, spending an estimated $1,000 every year to store things they don't need! Again, how ridiculous does that sound? As well as saving yourself a few dollars, you can also earn some money by selling the things you don't need.

CREATIVITY WILL FLOW

Having an organized environment frees your mind to become more relaxed and focused. When your surroundings are orderly, your brain is not forced to work so hard. On the other hand, when your environment is disorganized and full of clutter, there is no room in your brain to think straight, because whether you realize it or not, your mind is focused more on the mess than on being creative and developing new ideas. Clutter affects your ability to be at your best, it destroys your concentration, and pulls your attention away from the things that are the most important. When there is disorder in your environment, you will always have that nagging feeling of the things that you have left undone instead of giving your undivided attention to doing what you really want to do.

YOU WILL HAVE LESS STRESS IN YOUR LIFE

You probably haven't connected the dots, but I guarantee you that the majority of stress in your life is related to your disorganized space and messy environment. According to the Centers for Disease Control, the majority of our medical bills are due to stress-related conditions. Your surroundings dictate your mood, and one of the most therapeutic life-changing things you can do is get organized!

Ninety percent of people in the United States claim that a disorganized home or work environment has a negative effect on their overall well-being. Sixty-five percent say that mess has a negative effect on their mental health. Forty-three percent say that it demotivates them, which then leads to them feeling depressed.

When you know where things are, you feel a sense of calm. Imagine how less complicated your life would be if you could find everything you needed at the right time. In fact, studies have found that there is a direct link between anxiety, depression, and clutter. Misplacing items, being late, missing appointments, and untidy rooms all play a huge role in stress and anxiety, all of which are the result of being disorganized.

Experts in the field of organization have even stated that their clients have ended bad relationships, quit jobs they were not happy in, lost weight, and replaced bad habits with good ones after decluttering their homes. Clearing your space enables you to see things clearly.

You'll be More Motivated to Achieve Your Dreams

As you have just read, mess demotivates people, and when your home is disorganized and untidy, it's hard to see past the mess and focus on what's really important. When everything is organized, things get done on time, which means you have more hours in the day to work on the goals that you want to achieve.

You Will Set the Standards for Your Family

Children are products of their environment—if you are sloppy, they are going to be sloppy. How can you ask your kids to keep their rooms tidy when the rest of the house is a mess? It doesn't make any logical sense. If you want your children to respect and obey you, it is very important that you are living the life that you want them to live. Parents will often attempt to instill certain values and ideals into their children, but they have yet to master those values and ideals. My father was like this. He was always telling us off for leaving things unfinished; however, as I grew older, I realized that we had acquired one of his bad habits—he would always start projects and never finish them. He knew that it was a bad habit, and I'm sure it didn't make him feel very good about himself, so instead of working to change it, he attempted to enforce it on us. It didn't work because subconsciously, we had learned that leaving projects undone was the norm. I had to make a conscious decision to break this habit, but it took me many years to do so.

It is essential that you set a good example for your children to follow so that when they grow older, they will not depart from what you have taught them. As well as setting a good example, it's not good for small children, especially babies, to crawl around clutter; in fact, it can be extremely dangerous.

You Will Sleep Better

Everyone loves a good night's rest; however, if the room that you spend the majority of your time is in disarray, sleep will evade you. The bedroom is designed for rest, and studies have found that people with clutter in the bedroom experience more disturbances while asleep. There is nothing more frustrating than staring at a pile of junk before you close your eyes. When the last thing you see before you close your eyes and turn off the light is a mess, then that's the first thing you see when you open your eyes. You are programming your mind to accept that chaos is the norm. And whether you realize it or not, it places an imprint on your subconscious mind and interrupts your sleep at night. When you climb into a bed with clean sheets and a tidy room, you experience the peace and harmony required to enable you to get a good night's sleep.

Your Relationships Will Improve

What do your friends know you for? Is it the one who is always late because they got stuck in traffic or couldn't find their keys? The one who no one likes going to their house because it always smells of cat pee? They might make a joke of it, but are these really characteristics that you want to be known for? The NAPO conducted a survey of 1,397 people and asked them how much time it would take to get their house ready for a dinner party. Ten percent of respondents said they would never invite anyone to their home for dinner because it was so untidy, and six percent said that their homes were so untidy that it would take more than 40 hours to get it ready! These statistics sound absolutely outrageous, but they are a reality for a lot of people.

What happens when someone shows up at your house unexpectantly? Or when there is a medical emergency and the paramedics need to come inside your house? You won't have the time to get things in order. If you feel embarrassed about the state of your home, it's time to get it cleaned up so that you can invite more people over and spend time with the people you love.

Your house doesn't need to look like a show home. Even if you live in a trailer, a neat and orderly environment makes for a pleasant experience when people come over to visit. My motto in life is to be ready for anything, you never know what's going to happen or who is going to turn up at your door.

There are so many more benefits to being organized but space won't allow me to write about all of them. However, I'm sure you get the message that happiness and peace of mind can be as simple as getting your house in order.

CHAPTER 4:

DECLUTTERING AND UNEXPECTED TRANSFORMATION

My parents were far from wealthy. I was raised in government housing that only had two bedrooms to shelter 8 people! Life was not easy, but we managed. Not surprisingly, the house was always a mess—with eight children in two rooms, that shouldn't come as much of a shock. All my clothes were second hand; I don't remember ever getting anything new. My father worked out of town most of the time, so it was just my mom and us children, and in between taking care of us and making sure we had food to eat and clean clothes to wear, she didn't have time for much else.

However, my mom was a very gifted cake maker. When we could afford to, she would make the most delicious cakes—not only were they tasty, they were also pretty because she could do things with icing that I had never seen before. Even though we were happy, my parents wanted more, they just didn't know how to get it. To cut a long story short, my mom went to a conference with a friend one day and one of the main lessons she learned from it was about the importance of organization. I was pretty young when the change started, but all I remember was that one day I woke up and the kitchen was clean. You see, she would always leave the dishes overnight and get them done throughout the day. From that day forward, I never came downstairs in the morning to an untidy kitchen.

Then she started waking up earlier and cleaning the house. Although we only had two rooms, she made sure everything was neat and organized. She created a space for each of us to keep our belongings. She threw things out, scrubbed the carpet, cleaned the windows, the walls, the car. By the time she had finished, the house looked brand new. Now that the house was in order and she had a regular routine going to make sure that it was kept that way, she had extra time on her hands, so she started to make more cakes. While we were at school, she would walk around the neighborhood and sell them. We suddenly had extra money. My mom was a master at her craft, and word soon got around about her cakes, and the next thing I knew, she had set up shop from the house. People would come from all over the place to buy my mom's cakes! Within two years we had enough money to buy a bigger house, my dad quit his job, they opened a shop, they became millionaires, and the rest is history.

The moral of the story is that order breeds success. When my mom started doing the dishes at night instead of leaving them until the morning, she had no idea it would lead to a multimillion-dollar business, but what it did do was motivate her to get the rest of the house organized, and then she realized that she had all this free time on her hands. You will never move to the next phase in your life until you can take care of the basics.

All my friends and family know that I have a passion for teaching about vision. The popular school of thought is that if you can see it in your mind's eye, you can believe it and achieve it. Nice principle, but there is more to it than that. I strongly believe there is a missing piece of the puzzle that success gurus are failing to teach—the universe/God/your personal higher power must be able to trust you before it will give you what you want. So anytime any of my friends are having difficulty accomplishing their goals, they will ask me where I think they are going wrong, and it is always something really simple.

Some friends of mine—let's call them the Smiths—were struggling financially, but they desperately needed a new car and they decided to dream big about it. The Smiths wanted a brand-new Honda Civic paid for in cash. They spoke affirmations over their dreams and goals, they had all types of side hustles going on, but nothing seemed to be working out. When they approached me about this, I asked them to take a look at their current car. Now, I had never paid it any attention prior to this, but when I did, I realized that the state of their old car was what was blocking them from getting a new one. It was an absolute mess, despicable to look at on the inside and out. People were so horrified with the dirt that they had used their fingers to carve out the words "PLEASE CLEAN ME I DON'T LIKE BEING DIRTY" across the side of the car!

So, I let the Smiths know that they were not going to get the car they were dreaming about until they cleaned up the car they were driving. I told them to act as if the car that they were driving was their new car to show their higher power that they could be trusted with the vehicle they wanted. If not, when they got their brand-new Honda Civic, it would end up looking like the same piece of junk they are driving now. Well, they took my advice and cleaned up the car and kept it clean. Within three months, they had a brand-new Honda Civic, just as they had dreamed!

The bottom line is that you are not going to get what you want until you can be faithful with what you've got. If you want a new house, job, or car, one of the most powerful strategies for success is to live as if you've already got what you want, put excellence into practice as you make your way to your desired destination. As a rule of thumb, if there is anything in your environment that you can't look at and say, "This is excellent," then fix it until it is excellent!

A Character of Excellence Opens the Door to Success

We live in a world where everything is given to us immediately. We make microwave meals or grab a hamburger from a fast food restaurant instead of cooking, we get liposuction instead of working out, we buy things on credit instead of saving for it, and the list is endless. Society has trained us to grab and go, so we have no patience to put the effort into what we really want. We go to school and are told to focus on choosing the right career path, but whatever happened to focusing on choosing the right character path? Today, it is rare to find qualities such as perseverance, determination, and attention to detail in a person. Whether it's at home or at work, we think we can get away with doing the bare minimum, but at the same time expect to see huge results. I am sorry to disappoint you, but life doesn't work like that. When you are faithful with the little that you have, and that means doing things like putting your best efforts forward even when you are working in a job that you hate, you will strategically place yourself on the pathway to success.

For example, if you are currently renting but want to own your own home, treat the rented accommodation as if it were the mansion you want to own. Don't leave the carpets stained because you know they don't belong to you, don't bang holes into the walls to hang your pictures up unless you are planning on fixing them before you leave. If you can't be trusted with someone else's property, why should you be trusted with your own?

So, to conclude this chapter, my personal lesson in success is to treasure what you have and finish what you start. It is essential that you take care of the small things you own if you want to acquire more, but it is equally as important to finish what you start. When projects are left incomplete, no matter how small, they take up both physical and mental space. When you have that irritating feeling that you need to finish painting that room, clean out the attic, donate those old clothes to charity, or pay the rest of those bills, they occupy mental space simply because they are not finished.

There is more to this than not finishing things around the house, it also extends to the things you should be doing in life such as opening a savings account, getting into shape, or finishing an online course. Whatever it is, unfinished projects steal your peace and drain your energy. When you procrastinate in the areas of life that might not seem important, you carry that same attitude into the important areas of your life.

CHAPTER 5:

CREATING A SENSE OF ORDER

Walking into a clutter-free, pristine, and streamlined room is a wonderful feeling! However, for the majority of people, this doesn't come naturally, but this doesn't mean you can't learn to create this sense of order. When it comes to organizing your home, the goal is to make it functional so that everyone knows where everything is at any given time. This is what will create the peaceful environment you are looking for.

Your aim should be to do everything with excellence, and that includes washing the dishes before you go to bed, making sure your car is in the best condition, and making your bed first thing in the morning. Whatever you do, no matter how small, do it to the best of your ability and you will begin to feel a sense of pride for yourself and your surroundings. So, let's get started with organizing your life!

Take Photos: You want to take photos so that you have something to remind you of where you don't want to go back to and to remind you of how far you've come.

Staying Motivated: One of the hardest things about getting your life in order is not the process but staying motivated. The bottom line is that no one wants to work hard; we want the easy way out. Most people would much rather spend their time watching soap operas on the couch eating milk and cookies, but that's not going to get you anywhere is it? During my organizing phase, I listened to motivational music and teachings by powerful public speakers such as Les Brown, Tony Robbins and Brian Tracy. Not only was I getting my life in order, but I was also learning some life-changing messages. I found that if I ever tried to get anything done without listening to something motivational, I was not as productive.

Set an Alarm: It's impossible for you to work all day without having a break. I used a tool called the Pomodoro method, in which you basically work for 25 minutes and then have a five-minute break. Do this four times, have a 10-minute break, and then go back to five-minute breaks. Repeat until the end of the day. The website I used was www.tomato-timer.com/. Together with the motivational music and teachings, this timer really helps you to focus, it's almost as if you are racing against time because you know you only have a short window to get something done before the timer goes off.

CREATIVE IDEAS FOR ORGANIZING
THE FOYER, THE BACKDOOR, OR THE ENTRYWAY

Anyone that comes into your home will pass through one of these areas first, which is why it's so important for them to be free of clutter. Imagine someone walking into your home for the first time and the first thing they are introduced to is a pile of mess! Not only is it embarrassing for you, but a messy home makes guests feel uncomfortable. I know what I'm like when I walk into an untidy house, I don't want to sit down in case I leave with my trousers a different color and neither do I want a drink in case I swallow a roach! Here are some ideas to organize these areas:

- Shoes, Baseball Caps, Umbrellas, etc.: Perhaps after you get rid of all those books you will have an empty bookshelf. Turn it into storage space and use it to house the random items that are usually left around the doorway.

- Coats, Car Keys, House Keys, Dog Leashes, Backpacks, etc.: Fix a few hooks to the backdoor and use them to hang up these items. Make it a rule that as soon as anyone enters the house, the first thing they must do is hang their belongings on one of these hooks.

- Gloves, Scarves, Newspapers, Sports Equipment, etc.: Baskets and bins are relatively cheap, so they won't break the bank. Give one to each family member and put their name on it. They are to put all their belongings into the bin when they return home. However, make sure that these bins and baskets are monitored because they've got overload potential. You don't want anything and everything stored in them; they are only for certain items. Make sure you are very specific about this.

Additional Tip: Some entryways have the potential to look quite solemn and uninviting. You know, the type of hallways that are so dark and gloomy that you are scared to get to the end of it because you don't know what's waiting at the other side! You can brighten it up by hanging a mirror on the wall or painting the area a light and fluffy color.

THE LIVING ROOM

Have you ever wondered why the living room is called the living room? It's because that's where we spend most of our time when we are in the house, so it would only make sense that it is well organized. It can be pretty easy to get this room organized.

- Games, Blankets, Pillows: People usually stuff these items behind the couch or have them piled up against a wall. Buy some storage bins and stash these items away.

- Remote Controls, Newspapers, Magazines: Do you have any shelves in your living room? If not, get some and use them to house these items.

- Cords and Phone Chargers: The living room floor is often overrun with cords and phone chargers. If you have a drawer attached to your coffee table, fold up your cords and tuck them into empty toilet rolls, you can then tuck them away neatly into a drawer.

THE BEDROOMS

Bedrooms can get very untidy because this is where we keep our clothes, shoes, belts, makeup, etc. Keep these rooms organized by doing the following.

Bed Linens: When you don't have any storage space, bed linens are left wherever they will fit. If you have an old dresser, before you throw it out, remove the drawers and use them to house bed linens. You can then slide the drawers neatly under the bed.

Writing Supplies, Books, Journals: Most people have a terrible habit of allowing these items to pile up around their bed. If you have a bedside table with a drawer, use the drawer to store these items instead of leaving them on the floor.

Decorative Pieces, Frames: Make use of your wall space and hang these items up. All you need to do is bang a few nails into the wall.

Work Supplies, Magazines: Purchase an ottoman and put it at the foot of your bed, you can use it to store these items.

Dirty Clothes: Are you guilty of allowing your dirty clothes to pile up on the floor behind the door? Not to worry, I was too! Use the space available on the back of your door to hang a laundry hamper that you can put your dirty clothes in.

Arranging Your Clothes: Before I started to get my life in order, my clothes were stuffed wherever they could fit. And when I needed to wear anything, I would pull everything out to find what I was looking for. I was constantly surrounded by piles of clothes until I learned how to fold and organize them properly.

Folding Button-Down Shirts

- Lay the shirt down on a flat surface (a bed or an ironing board will do)
- Button the shirt from the top down, but leave the cuffs open
- Turn the shirt over and stretch the arms out to the sides
- Fold one arm over so that the shirt is folded in half
- Fold the same arm at an angle back on itself
- Do the same to the other side

How to Fold a Sweater

- Lay the sweater face up on a flat surface
- Use your hands to smooth out any wrinkles
- Fold the sleeves across the front of the sweater so they end up touching the base of the sweater
- Take the bottom of the sweater and fold it up towards the neck

How to Fold a T-Shirt

- Lay the t-shirt out on a flat surface
- Use your hands to smooth out any wrinkles

- Fold the t-shirt in half long ways
- Fold the sleeves backward and smooth them over
- Take the bottom of the t-shirt and fold it up to the end of the sleeves
- Fold the collar down on top of the sleeves

How to Fold Jeans

- Put your hand into each pocket and make sure they are pushed down
- Hold the jeans at the waist and shake them out
- Lay them out onto a flat surface
- Fold one leg on top of the other and use your hands to smooth out any wrinkles
- Make sure both legs are perfectly lined up
- Pick the legs up from the bottom and fold them up to the waist
- Fold the jeans again by doing the same

How to Fold a Skirt

- If the skirt has pockets, use your hands to make sure the pockets are pushed down
- Lay the skirt on a flat surface and smooth out any wrinkles
- Fold the bottom of the skirt up towards the waist
- Fold the skirt again corner to corner
- Do this one more time depending on the size of the skirt

HOW TO ORGANIZE YOUR CLOSET

Before you start organizing your closet, the first thing you need to do is go through your clothes and get rid of anything you don't wear. If you haven't worn an item of clothing in a year or more, you don't wear it! You can either donate them, sell them, or give them to a friend. Whatever you do, just get rid of them!

Storage baskets: If there is anything you can't store away neatly, put them into a storage basket. If you don't have any, they are pretty cheap to buy.

Use all Available Space: If you have a spare wall in your closet, fix a towel bar to it, and hang your scarves and belts on it.

Use a Boot Organizer: Boots can be difficult in a closet. They fall over at the slightest touch and, eventually, you just get fed up and leave them on the floor. A boot organizer hangs from the clothes rack and each boot is attached to its own clip.

Add Your Dressing Table: If you have enough space, you can create more room in your bedroom by putting your dresser and mirror in the closet.

Arrange Shoes on the Door: This idea only works for heels—screw towel rails on the back of the door and hang your shoes on them.

Use Shelf Dividers: Instead of lumping everything to-gether on the top shelf, use shelf dividers to separate your folded clothes.

Add Another Bar: Once you've gotten rid of the clothes you don't wear, and you still don't have enough room, dou-ble up your space by adding another bar in the closet.

Use Good Hangers: If you use those old wire hangers, it's time to get rid of them, they make your closet look un-kempt. Buy metal slim open hangers, not only are they stur-dy and look better, they make it easier to get your clothes off the rack.

A Higher Rod: If you don't have enough space in your closet for two rods, hang the one that you've got higher up. This will create more space for you to put something un-derneath, like a shoe rack or a dresser.

Hats, Socks, Gloves, etc.: These small items can become overwhelming when you have too many of them. Fruit bas-kets are great for putting these items in and using vertical space.

Sweaters: Sweaters are so big and bulky that they just take up too much space; get them out of the way by rolling them up and slotting them into the cubbies of a hanging shoe organizer.

Scarves: Take a single hanger and attach shower hooks to it and then neatly hang your scarves over them.

Underwear: Prevent your underwear from getting lost in the back of the drawer by storing them in shoeboxes.

Purses: Hang wire baskets fastened to the back of the closet door. Command hooks are a good way to store purses, handbags, and other accessories.

THE BATHROOM

This is another room in the house where guests will definitely visit, so it is essential to keep it well organized at all times. Also, you will find that it is easier to get ready in the mornings when the bathroom is tidy.

- Hair ties, Brushes, and Combs: Most people have drawers in their bathroom, and they just stuff things in there, which means they have to rummage through a pile of junk to get to anything. Keep the drawer organized by putting a kitchen utensil tray in it and arranging these items in each compartment.

- Hair Tools: Store items such as flat irons, curling irons, and blow driers in a magazine holder.

- Nail Polish: You can either purchase a nail polish shelf or store your nail polish collection in cookie jars, depending on how many you have. You can separate them into colors in different jars. If you really want to get creative, you can use a spice rack.

- Bobby Pins: The next time you buy a packet of Tic Tac's, don't throw away the empty container, use them to store your bobby pins.

- Lipstick: Instead of piling your lipsticks up in a bathroom drawer, arrange them in miniature loaf or muffin pans.

- Makeup: Ok, so I know I have spent the majority of this book telling you to get rid of stuff, but there are a few things that can come in handy for storage such as your daughter's old bead organizer. They have great compartments for women to fit all their make up in. If not, purchase a makeup stand from your local supermarket.

- Perfumes: Save some space in your bathroom by using a 2-tiered cake tray to show off your perfume collection.

- Cleaning Products: Instead of leaving them on the floor around the toilet, put your cleaning products into a bucket and store them under the sink.

- Medicine: All family members should know where the medicine cabinet is. It should be stored in one location in the bathroom instead of multiple different places, which is usually the case. You can attach small storage bins to the inside of your cabinet door and arrange the medicine in them.

- Towels: Organize your towels by size, sets, and color. Fold them neatly and arrange them in drawers, storage boxes, or on shelves.

- Vanity: Your countertop should be as empty as possible. Not only does this look neater, but it also makes it easier to clean. If you have run out of drawer and cabinet space, make sure you display the nicest items on your countertops.

JEWELRY

- Necklaces: Eliminate messy piles of necklaces by hanging them individually onto a pegboard.

- Bracelets: Neatly stack bracelets onto a paper towel holder.

- Earrings: Stop your small earrings from getting lost and mixed up by arranging them in an ice cube tray.

THE KITCHEN

- Produce: Once again, this is where some of your old items come in handy. Hang an old shower caddy on the inside of the pantry door or on the side of the cabinet to store things like peppers and onions.

- Soup Cans: Wire baskets are great for stacking soup or any other type of cans. They allow you to keep the labels visible and they make cans easier to stack.

- Cutting Boards: Wire bins come in very handy when it comes to storing cutting boards. Attach one to the back of the cabinet door.

- Long Handled Utensils: If you have an old flower vase, use it to store your tall utensils in and arrange it on top of the counter.

- Boxed Goods: You can cut down on storage space in the pantry by using clear canisters and emptying your boxed goods such as cereal and rice into them.

- Plastic Wrap, Tin Foil, and Sandwich Bags: A cardboard magazine holder is excellent for storing these items. They keep them organized and make them easy to grab hold of when needed.

- Tea Bags: Tea bags should be kept in a closed container to keep them fresh. Store them in see-through mason jars with airtight lids.

- Plastic Tupperware Lids: Are you forever buying new Tupperware because you are always losing the lids? Store them in a metal cooling rack attached to a basket to keep them from growing legs and going on the run.

- Cleaning Products: Free up some space on your cabinet floor by hanging your cleaning products on a tension rod under the sink.

Oven Drawers: Do me a favor, go and open your oven drawer. I guarantee you will find nothing in there that's oven related. We toss everything in there to keep the area free from clutter, but then we end up making an even bigger mess; but because we can't see it, we think it's ok.

It's not a big drawer; actually, its most likely the smallest drawer in the kitchen, neither is it easy to access. This is one of the reasons you tend to throw everything in there, you don't think anyone will ever see it. However, there is the proper use for everything in the kitchen, and that includes the oven drawer. If you can manage it, the best way to de-clutter an oven drawer is to keep it empty. If not, keep it to these items only:

- Flat items: Store flat items such as baking pans and lids in one half of the oven drawer. Don't keep them in the middle or you will make a mess when looking for other items.

- Lids: In general, pots are stackable, which means you are left with finding somewhere to put the lids. Store them in the oven drawer for easy access.

The Plastic Bag Issue: Plastic bags can become a real problem. Most of us go grocery shopping on a weekly basis, and instead of recycling bags, we tend to accumulate more every week! To eliminate this problem, put the majority of your plastic bags in the recycling bin. Keep 5 large bags and 10 small bags, then store them somewhere you will have easy access to them.

- Old milk carton: Cut the top off a milk carton and wash it out. Stuff the plastic bags in them and store them in the cupboard under the sink or in a place that's convenient for you.

- An empty tissue box: An empty tissue box is ready to use. Place the plastic bags inside the box and store them in the cupboard under the sink or in a place that's convenient for you.

- A pantyhose leg: Cut the leg off one of your old pantyhose, stuff the plastic bags inside, and hang it up inside a cupboard, in the pantry, or a place that's convenient for you.

Sink and Dish Area: It's easy for this area to become cluttered, kids leave their dishes in the sink, and before you know it, there's a big mess. You can avoid this by doing the following:

- If you have a dishwasher, make sure the dishes are stacked here instead of left on the sides or in the sink.

- If you don't have a dishwasher, leave a dish rack in the sink. When it gets full, you will know it's time to get your rubber gloves on and do some washing up.

THE LAUNDRY ROOM

Laundry rooms are typically pretty small, and with limited space you want to make sure the space that you do have is well utilized.

- Bleach, Dryer Sheets, Detergent: If you don't have cabinets in your laundry room, a hanging storage rack is a great option. You can also install shelves above the washer and dryer to store your supplies. The back of the door is often an overlooked storage space, you can hang a shoe organizer over it and use it to store your appliances.

- The Ironing Board: Hide the ironing board by hanging it on coat hooks behind the door.

THE PLAY ROOM

Kids love their playroom, and they also know how to keep it looking a hot mess! Get your children's playroom organized by doing the following:

- Toys: There is not really much point in organizing toys because they are going to get messed up quickly. Before your kids start playing, lay a blanket on the floor and dump the toys on top. When they have finished playing, pull the blanket together and put the toys back into the storage bin.

- Dolls: Hang a shoe organizer over the back of the door and store all dolls, action figures, and barbies.

- Puzzles: Empty puzzle pieces into Ziplock bags and throw the boxes away.

- Stuffed Animals: Hang a hammock or a plastic chain from the ceiling and attach all your child's stuffed animals.

- Board Games: If you don't have any already, install shelves to the walls and place all board games on them.

- Books: Does your child have an old wagon? Use it to store all their storytime books.

THE OFFICE

Not every home has an office; but if you do, this is how to keep it organized:

Files: Get rid of all your manila folders and replace them with color-coded ones. This will allow you to immediately find what you need. To get used to the system, you might want to write a list and stick it to the wall. For example: Green = Bills, Blue = Insurance, etc.

Desk Essentials: The spice rack has so many different uses and one of them is to store your office supplies. Use spice containers to house post-it notes, rubber bands, thumb tacks, paper clips, etc.

THE GARAGE

Think about this for a minute: the random items taking up so much space in your garage are worth very little in comparison to the expensive car that's sitting in the driveway! Is that not incentive enough to get your garage in order?

- Beach Balls, Soccer Balls, Basket Balls: Corral these items against the wall with bungee cords.

- Miscellaneous Items: Garages are full of random items, such as tacks, nails, pins, and rubber bands. Get them out the way by storing them in a muffin pan; the small compartments will allow you to easily store these items.

- Nuts and Bolts: A great way to get those nuts and bolts out the way is to store them in a spice rack.

- Tools: Attach a towel bar to the wall and then attach hooks to them, you can then hang tools such as garden hoses and rakes and spades.

THE CAR

Most people never think about getting their car in order because they don't spend a lot of time in it. Here is how you can make it a bit more organized.

- Tissues, Snacks, Hand Sanitizers: A great way to store these items is to drape mesh or plastic shower pockets over the back of the front car seats. This gives the kids easy access to these things, and they can put them back when they're finished instead of leaving them on the floor.

- Cups, Toys: A plastic caddy is great for storing miscellaneous items during your journey.

That's pretty much it guys. You don't need to utilize all the suggestions but pick the ones that are best suited to your living space. Remember, organization and cleanliness keeps you focused, your mind clear, your concentration sharp, and most of all, it makes you feel good. It's going to take a while to get all this done, but once it's complete, you will feel on top of the world.

CHAPTER 6:

---

30 DAY KNOCK OUT CHALLENGE

I think you've read enough now, it's time to get moving! By now, I hope you know what you need to do to get your life organized. In what areas do you feel as if your life is spiraling out of control? Take a look at your surroundings, what does your clutter say about you? Where are you taking on too much? Why do you think you have accumulated the number of things that you have? Thinking about this stuff is overwhelming, I know, I have been there; however, this step is essential if you are going to move forward.

It is in no way going to take you 30 days to declutter your home, but the aim is to get things done in 30-day increments.

Step 1: Planning is an important part of life—if you don't know where you are going, how are you going to get there? A plan is like a detailed roadmap that tells you how to get to your destination. Decide where you are going to start first. I chose the messiest room in the house. I thought if I can get that done then I can do anything, and I was certainly right.

Step 2: Write down a list of the top 10 things that need to be done in the room that you have been putting off. For example, folding the laundry, getting the bills in order, etc.

Step 3: Now attack this list with a 30-day knockout challenge! Get your calendar and block out the next 30 days with everything that you need to do. So, for example, July 1 might say: Organize shoes, fold clothes. Make up your mind to ensure that everything you include on this list is completed within the 30 days. As you get through with each one, tick them off as you go along. Believe me when I say you will be absolutely fired up and motivated once you get to the end of the 30 days. You will realize that you have completed everything you set out to. You will want to kick yourself for taking so long in the first place, which will give you the drive, motivation, and the confidence to achieve bigger goals.

As you begin to transform your home and live a life of excellence in every area, it will show, and people will start to notice, admire, and respect you. Instead of feeling drained from the mess you were forced to look at every day, you will feel energetic, enthusiastic, and excited about life. No longer will you be controlled by your circumstances, but you will have full control over them, and you will start to run towards the destiny that you know you deserve.

Don't let the miniscule things in your life drown out the things that are the most important. Develop a mental attitude that is determined to get things done no matter how large or small.

TURN YOUR TRASH INTO CASH

As you have read, excess items in the home are a waste of money. The good news is that it's not all doom and gloom; you can turn some of your trash into cash. Remember that one man's trash is another man's treasure! What you don't use someone else will.

A recent survey found that over half of the employees who participated said that saving more money was on the top of the list for their New Year resolution; however, less than 69% of Americans have $1,000 in savings. You have also read that Americans love to waste money storing items they don't need, contributing to the multi-billion dollar per year storage industry. If you are guilty of owning a storage unit, go empty it right now!

eBay conducted a survey and found that the average household stores over 50 unused items worth approximately $3,100. Just think about what you could do with that extra money! Once you have decided what you are going to throw away and what you are going to keep, set another 30-day challenge to sell the items. Whatever you can't sell, donate. The idea here is to get the things that you don't need out of your house and into the hands of the people that do need them.

Decide how much money you want to make from your items, and make sure you stick to it. You see, once you get your stuff online and you open the door for people to contact you, there are going to be people who will want to trade stuff. In other words, instead of paying for it, they will want to give you something else that is of the same value. Do not get sucked into this game because some of these deals can be quite tempting. Remember, your aim is to make money from the items you want to get rid of, not gain more items. Think about what you will be able to do with the money: pay off credit card bills, pay down a car note, or put the money into savings.

It is also important to mention that the decluttering process is not just about getting rid of things you don't want, it's also about getting rid of the things you don't use—you know, all those items that are lurking in the back of the closet that you fantasize about using one day! A rule of thumb to go by is to get rid of anything that hasn't been used in 12 months or more.

How to Turn Your Trash into Cash

You are probably thinking, "Well this sounds like a great idea, but how do I go about doing it?" Not to worry, I'm about to show you how.

Selling Tips

Selling your unused and unwanted items is a great idea, but you need to know what you are doing before you start. Here are a few tips to get you started:

Do Some Research: If you've got some expensive pieces like electronic goods, go online and find out how much they are selling brand new and then price them at slightly cheaper. For example, if you have a phone that's worth $350, sell it for $275. You are selling the items cheaper than they are worth because, even though you may not have used them, they are considered second hand. You also want to give buyers an incentive to purchase from you. You can also check sites like eBay and Amazon to find out the going rates for your items.

Descriptions: If you choose to sell your items online, it is essential that you give an accurate description of the product. If the speaker has scratches on it, let potential buyers know. At the end of the day, if you are not honest about the condition, the buyer has the right to return it and request a refund. You can avoid this by being upfront from the start. You also want to make sure that you take good pictures of the items against a clear background. For example, if you are selling a black phone, photograph it against a white background.

Prime Time Posting: According to research, the best time to list items on an auction site is between the hours of 7:00 pm to 9:00 pm (CST). However, the times might be different for your local area, so do some research before posting.

THE BEST ITEMS TO SELL

There are certain items that are in higher demand than others; for example, you might not get very far trying to sell a box of paperclips, but clothing and electronics will sell better. Here are some of the most popular items to sell:

Books: How many novels and textbooks do you have that you no longer read. Instead of them collecting dust, sell them and collect some cash. www.bookriot.com will give you a list of the best sites to sell books, or you can sell them to your local bookstore.

CDs and DVDs: CDs and DVDs are a thing of the past; most people have an ancient pile stacked up in the corner of their living room. You can sell your CDs and DVDs on websites such as www.ziffit.com.

Gift Cards: They sound like an odd thing to sell, but they sell; you might have been given some gift cards as a gift, but you haven't used them and don't intend to. Studies have found that approximately $750 million in gift cards a year are never redeemed! That's a lot, but I'm guilty of doing the same. Consider selling your gift cards for cash, especially when it's a gift card from a store you are not particularly fond of. You can get some decent money for your gift cards or you can exchange them for cash on sites such as www.cardcash.com/sell-gift-cards/ and www.cardpool.com.

Clothes: You don't need a closet full of designer clothes to be able to sell them. You will be surprised at what people will buy at a discounted price. You can sell the clothes you no longer wear on sites like www.amazon.com, www.eBay.com, and www.etsy.com.

Furniture: The best places to sell your furniture are antique malls, consignment shops, and a garage sale.

Electronics: www.yourenew.com, www.buybackworld.com, www.gazelle.com, and www.usell.com are just a few sites that will buy your electronic goods for cash. These include desktop computers, phones, digital cameras, laptops, iPods, and much more.

Refrigerators and Air Conditioning Units: How many of you have an old refrigerator or air conditioning unit collecting cobwebs in the back of the shed? Well did you know that your local energy company will take these items off your hands at no cost to you and give you cash for them in return?

Musical Instruments: My kids wanted all sorts of music lessons when they were younger, but as they grew into their teenage years they were no longer interested, so we had a pile of musical instruments in the house. I am sure some of you can relate to this, it was a waste of money; some music stores and pawn shops will pay you decent money for your unwanted musical instruments.

Jewelry: Has your boyfriend just dumped you? Don't waste your time or energy mourning over the breakup, cash in on that ring, necklace, or bracelet he bought you. You can sell your jewelry on sites such as www.never-likeditanyway.com and www.idonowidont.com. They will give you top dollar for them too!

GET SELLING!

Now that you know what to sell, it's time to start selling! Here are some great ways to sell your unused items.

Garage Sale: Get a flyer made up, it doesn't need to be anything fancy, take some pictures of some of the best items you want to sell, paste them onto a word document and provide details of the garage sale, location, time, a list of the items, etc. Get the kid, (if you don't have any, do it yourself) and go around town handing out these fliers. Put them in letterboxes, leave them in stores, hairdressers, and pin them up on bus stop windows. The point is to let the entire town know that you are having a garage sale! You won't get the highest prices with a garage sale because people expect bargains, but it will help you to get rid of the majority of your stuff.

Pawn Shops: If you have a lot of old electronics and jewelry and you don't want to deal with the hassle of selling them yourself, take them to a pawn shop. They will gladly take them off your hands. Again, you won't get the highest prices because they have to sell them and make a profit, but you will get something.

The Internet: One of the main benefits of selling your items online is that you get to put them in front of a global audience which means you have a higher chance of selling them because more people will be scoping your stuff! The best sites to use are eBay.com, Amazon.com, Etsy.com, and a phone app called LetGo. LetGo is an app geared for local selling and buying. The plus side is you don't have to worry about shipping, and shipping costs, as people just come to pick up your stuff! Just make sure that you use discretion when selling to strangers, and meet in a public place when you're ready to sell. There are tons more, but these are the best. There is no complicated sign-up process, simply load up a picture and a description of the items you want to sell, sit back and wait for the bids to come rolling in!

Auctions: This is only for people who have some really rare and antique items; you won't get very far trying to sell the sewing machine you don't use at an auction. To find out how much your items might be worth, you can visit an online auction site or go to your local auction house if there is one in your area.

Consignment Shops: Do you have any designer clothes you don't wear? Or any expensive furniture? If so, take them to a consignment shop and they will gladly take them off your hands. There are also consignment shops that take toys, video games, children and baby clothes. Consignment shops basically sell your items for you, they sell them at the highest price possible and split the profits with you.

Social Media: If you don't want to sell your items to random people, advertise your things on your social media profiles and sell them to friends and family instead.

CHAPTER 7:

ENVIRONMENTALLY FRIENDLY CLEANING METHODS

Once you have gotten rid of what you don't need in each room, the next step is cleaning! Before you start rearranging things, you want to make sure that the area is clean. I am a huge fan of using natural products to clean. Not only are they better for your health, but they are also better for the environment. We have been fooled into believing that the only way to remove grime, grease, and dirt is by using harsh chemicals. This is so not true! I have been making my own natural cleaning products for years, and I can tell you that they work even better than the commercial stuff. I remember the last time I used store-bought cleaning products. I bent over the bathtub and started spraying what I was using at the time. I had to squint my eyes because I could feel the burn. I assumed this was normal, as I had been using these products for so many years, but something clicked at that moment and I just thought to myself, "There is no way this can be safe." My eyes were burning, my nose was running, and I was coughing—that's not healthy! So, I started looking into the negative effects of store-bought cleaning products and I was very disturbed at what I found. May I add, I wasn't reading random blogs by people who have a love for the planet, what I found came from professional and credible sources. One of them was the Cancer Prevention Coalition (CPC). They have conducted several studies and found that the majority of American household cleaning products contain a high level of carcinogenic and toxic ingredients. It has also been found that most of these ingredients cause cancer!

- Lysol Disinfectant Spray is mixed with an ingredient called "orthophenylphenol" (OPP). Research has found that this product causes bladder tumors.

- Ajax Cleanser is made up of an ingredient called "crystalline silica," which causes skin, eye, and lung irritation.

- Ortho Weed Killer contains an ingredient called "Dichlopophenoxyacetate," which causes lymphoma, cancer, and soft tissue sarcoma.

After this shocking discovery, I started looking for alternatives, and my search led me to products that I could start using immediately because they were sitting in my cupboard! These included baking soda, lemon juice, and vinegar!

Here are some house cleaning tips using natural products that will turn your home into the palace it was destined to be!

CLEANING YOUR LIVING ROOM

Cleaning your sofa and cushions: Before you start, check the care tag to ensure that it has a "W" written on it. This means that you can self-clean your sofa without ruining it. If not, you will need to contact a professional to clean it for you.

- Fill a bucket with lukewarm water
- Add half a cup of white vinegar
- Add one spoon of baking powder
- Use a long wooden spoon to stir and combine
- Dip a sponge into the mixture and squeeze out the excess water
- Start cleaning the cushions first and rub the sponge over both sides
- Once clean, put them up against a wall to dry
- To keep them from touching, place clean towels or kitchen paper towels between them
- To clean the sofa, take it apart and use the same cleaning process for the cushions
- Let the sofa air dry
- Make sure the sofa and cushions are completely dry before putting them back together

How to Clean Leather Chairs
- Add 1/3 of white vinegar to a glass jar
- Add 2/3 of olive oil
- Put a lid on the jar and shake it vigorously to combine the ingredients

- Take a dry cloth and pour out some of the mixture onto it
- Use the cloth to buff the chairs

How to Get Rid of Pet Smells from Your Sofa

- Pull your sofa apart and air dry it outside for as long as possible.

  Use a carpet beater or a stick to beat out the salt residue remaining from urine
- Sprinkle a generous amount of baking soda over the couch parts and let it sit for the night
- Vacuum the sofa the next day

HOW TO CLEAN YOUR DINING ROOM

The dining table is the most important part of the dining room. They come in a variety of materials, sizes, and shapes. Once damaged, they can be very expensive to repair, so here are some tips to restore and clean your dining table.

How to Disguise Scratches

- Select a nut that is the same or similar in color to your dining table—a walnut works well
- In a horizontal direction, rub the nut over the scratch
- Darken the scratch by dipping a cotton swab in iodine and going over the scratch
- You may need to repeat the above step several times to get the color to match

How to Remove Smudges

- Fill a large bowl with lukewarm water
- Add half a cup of white vinegar
- Soak a cotton cloth in the liquid squeeze out the excess
- Wipe over the area

How to Clean a Glass Table

- Add one tablespoon of white vinegar to a spray bottle
- Add one cup of water
- Add one cup of rubbing alcohol
- Shake the spray bottle vigorously
- Spray the glass table and use a lint-free cloth to wipe over it

HOW TO CLEAN THE BATHROOM

We use the bathroom daily, so it has the potential to get the dirtiest. Mildew, trapped hair in the drain, a smelly toilet, and whatever else you can think of makes it a very unpleasant place to clean, yet it has to be done. Not only do you visit the bathroom daily, but it is the one room that your guests are most likely to visit, so it's important to keep the bathroom clean at all times.

How to Clean the Inside of the Toilet

- In a large bowl, combine one tablespoon of baking soda with half a cup of white vinegar

- Pour this mixture into the toilet bowl making sure it goes around the sides
- Leave the mixture for 30 minutes
- Use a toilet brush to scrub the bowl
- Flush the toilet

How to Clean the Outside of the Toilet

- In a spray bottle mix one-part vinegar with three parts water and one part baking soda
- Give the bottle a good shake
- Spray the entire toilet bowl
- Let it sit for around 10 minutes
- Use a damp cloth to remove the dirt and the solution

How to Remove Limescale From the Toilet

If the limescale is above the waterline, gently scrape it off with a butter knife. If it is below the waterline, push the water down with a toilet brush and then scrape. If the limescale is on the base of the toilet bowl, you will need to remove the water with a cup before scraping. Once you have managed to get rid of the limescale, flush the toilet.

For really stubborn limescale, fill the toilet with half a gallon of vinegar and leave it overnight. In the morning use a toilet brush to scrub the bowl and then flush.

Cleaning Your Sink's Drain

- Wearing gloves, remove the covering and pull out any gunk and hair from the drain

- Pour 3/4 cup of baking soda down the sink hole
- Pour 1/2 a cup of white vinegar down the sink hole
- Use a stopper to block the drain for 30 minutes
- Boil some water, remove the stopper, and pour it down the drain

How to Clean the Toilet Waste Pipe

If you have never cleaned your toilet waste pipe, let me warn you, you are in for a nasty surprise!

- Soak a damp cloth in vinegar
- Use the cloth to scrub the pipe
- For difficult stains soak the cloth in vinegar and wrap it around the pipe and let it sit for 30 minutes before wiping

How to Remove Soap Scum

- Create a paste by combining baking soda and dish liquid
- Soak a sponge or a cloth in the mixture
- Scrub at the soap scum until it dissolves
- Soak a cloth in warm water and wipe the area clean

How to Remove Mold

- Pour white vinegar into a spray bottle
- Spray the mold and leave it to dry
- Spray the mold again and use a damp cloth to remove the mold

You might have to do this a few times to get rid of the mold. You can prevent the buildup of mold by spraying the bath or shower with a water and vinegar mix daily.

How to Clean the Shower Curtain

You can clean vinyl or plastic shower curtains in several ways. If the curtain is not too dirty, simply spray it with a combination of vinegar and water and then clean it with a damp cloth. For a more thorough clean, soak a sponge in water, sprinkle it with baking powder, and then give the curtain a good scrub. If you've neglected your shower curtain for a while and it's infested with mildew, you will need to take the curtain outside. Lay it on the ground and scrub it with baking soda and vinegar. If all else fails, put the curtain in the washing machine and add ½ a cup of baking soda into the detergent, wash it with a few towels to help remove the dirt.

Cleaning Your Shower Head and Removing Limescale

- Add 2 cups of vinegar to a bucket
- Fill the bucket with water
- Remove the shower head and place it in the bucket—leave it overnight

Removing Limescale from the Sink

- Scrape the limescale buildup using a butter knife being careful not to scrape too hard or you will damage the porcelain

- Wipe around the sink with a damp cloth
- For really tough stains, add one cup of baking soda and one cup of vinegar to a bowl and stir it together to form a paste
- Lather it around the sink and leave it for an hour
- Rinse the sink and then wipe it with a cloth

How to Clean Bathroom Mirrors

- Fill a spray bottle with warm soapy water
- Wipe the mirror off using paper from a magazine or a sheet of newspaper
- Buff with a dry sheet of paper

How to Clean the Bathtub

- Combine one part white vinegar, one part baking soda, and one part water in a bucket
- Stir to combine
- Soak a sponge in the mixture and scrub the tub with the hard side of the sponge
- Once the entire tub has been cleaned, rinse it with water

HOW TO CLEAN YOUR BEDROOM

Your bed is the most important part of your bedroom. To keep the room and your bedding presentable, change your bedding every week. Not only will this give your bedroom that extra glow, but it will also preserve your bed linen. Pillowcases have the tendency to get dirty really quickly, so you will need to change them twice a week. Wash your comforter once a month.

How to Clean Bedspreads and Blankets

Check the label to see whether you will need to dry clean your bedspreads or blankets. In most cases, you can put them in the washing machine.

Satin or silk bedding is slightly different and will probably need to go to the dry cleaners. Washing them on the wrong temperature or with the wrong detergent will ruin them.

To get rid of stains on your cotton sheets, dip the stain into lemon juice and then put them in the washing machine.

If you have a king-sized bed with large bedding, I suggest taking it to the launderette to get a proper wash. When domestic washing machines are overloaded, they don't do the best of jobs.

How to Clean Blankets

Most people are unaware that blankets collect dust, which is a major contributor to allergies. To get rid of dust, vacuum them every two weeks and then hang them over a clothesline to air. You can then put them in the washing machine.

CHAPTER 8:

DECLUTTERING YOUR RELATIONSHIPS – GETTING RID OF NEGATIVE FRIENDS

There is more to being a minimalist than getting your house and car in order. Messy relationships can weigh you down just as much as a messy house. Negative friends can rob you of your peace of mind, happiness, and your ability to move forward in life and achieve your goals. Have you ever heard the saying "misery loves company?" Well, once your negative friends see that you are trying to change your life for the better, they will do everything in their power to drag you down. Positive and negative don't mix, and unless your friends want to change too, there is no point in staying in the relationship because you will quickly revert back to your old ways. Think about it like this, imagine standing on a table and trying to pull someone up to stand on it with you. It's impossible. They will end up pulling you down, and that's what happens with negative friends when you attempt to walk in a different direction. You desperately want them to come on your journey with you, but they are not ready to make that change so you try to pull them up, but they end up pulling you down. Here are five reasons you need to get rid of negative friends if you want to successfully declutter your life.

1. Negative Friends Don't Have Your Best Interests at Heart

The main aim of a friendship is to empower each other, not drag each other down. Friends are supposed to assist you in getting to the next level in life; therefore, it is important that you associate with people who are of the same mindset as you.

Negative friends don't really care about you as a person. All they care about is themselves, and they will drain your energy, making sure that their needs are always met at your expense. They don't care about how you might be feeling or what you might be going through when they decide that they want your help; their main concern is that they get what they want.

2. Negative Friends Drain Your Energy

Negative friends always have some drama going on in their lives that they need you to assist them with. They are extremely pessimistic and they always have something negative to say about the positive advice you attempt to give them. Because they are so negative, they attract negative situations in their lives, hence the constant drama that you end up getting caught up in because you're their friend. These people don't lift you up, they bring you down, and when you are around them you feel as though you are being suffocated by a cloud of negative black smoke. These are not the type of people you want in your life. You need to be around people who are going to encourage you to become the best version of yourself and achieve the goals you have set. If you feel depleted any time you are around certain friends, you are going to have to get rid of them.

3. **Negative Friends Don't Want You to Succeed**

Have you ever told a friend about something you hoped to achieve and all they could do was discourage you with statements like, "Are you sure this is a good idea? It sounds really risky," or "There are too many problems, I don't think you will be able to overcome them."

Or they try to guilt-trip you by saying things like, "What about me? I thought we would ride or die forever."

Statements like this are not encouraging you to succeed, they are encouraging you to stay in the predicament you are in so that you will never move forward in life. Negative friends are so selfish. All they care about is themselves, so much so that when it comes to your plans for the future, they think they have the right to be included, and if they are not, then you are the bad guy for abandoning them.

4. **Your Potential for Greatness is at Risk**

As you have just read, negative friends will do everything in their power to prevent you from becoming successful in life. Once they can see that you are actively taking steps to better yourself, they become like crabs in a bucket and try to pull you back down. Such people can rob you of your chance to become great. You see, it's easier to be negative than to be positive. The world is in total chaos; all you have to do is turn on the TV or open a newspaper and all you see is doom and gloom. Negative friends will remind you of everything that's wrong with the world, wrong with you, and wrong with them. All of which is an attempt to get you to give up on your dreams. Their ultimate goal is to convince you that the world is hopeless and so are you, so there is simply no point in trying.

It is essential that you let go of anyone who is opposed to where you want to go in life. Oil and water don't mix, neither do negative and positive—it's either one or the other! It will be impossible for you to become a positive person and live your best life with negative friends. You put yourself in harm's way when you surround yourself with people who are not walking in the same direction as you.

5. **Negative People Will Ruin Your Reputation**

Have you ever heard the saying that birds of a feather flock together? Well, if you hang around with negative Nancy's, people are going to assume you are the same way. When you decide to change your life, it's not that you think you are now better than your friends, you have just come to the realization that if you want to succeed in life then you are going to have to change your attitude. Once you change your attitude, you also need to change your friends to suit your new attitude. One thing you don't want is to ruin your chances of making new positive friends because you won't let go of negative friends. Positive people want to be around positive people.

As you have read this, you have probably come to the realization that there are a few people in your life that you need to get rid of, and this is not an easy task. At the end of the day, there is a possibility that you have been friends with such people since high school, and it's simply not that easy to cut them out of your life. But let me tell you, if you don't, the universe will. Here's an example.

My older sister (we'll call her Jessica) is an artist. She is 42 years old and had been best friends with a girl (we'll call her Sandy) since she was 18; they went to high school together. Sandy is a party girl. She is very self-centered, loves attention, and is always in a bad relationship that revolves around an insane amount of drama. Sandy went out every weekend and dragged my sister along with her; however, when my sister decided that it was time to get serious with her art, the dynamics of their relationship changed. Jessica could no longer spend as much time with Sandy as she used to, and Sandy didn't like it. To cut a long story short, Sandy decided to make other friends so she could continue her party life. One day, Sandy invited Jessica out with her new friends, for old times' sake she decided to go, and it was a complete disaster!

My sister was not the same person and was no longer interested in fruitless gossip and the drama that surrounded Sandra's life. Her new friends were exactly the same as Sandy and didn't like Jessica's positive vibes. Whenever she attempted to change the conversation, they would get irate and accuse my sister of being a killjoy. That night they had a massive argument and haven't spoken since. A twenty plus-year friendship was destroyed in one night because my sister had decided to take a different direction in life. The good news is that since their split, she has become a very successful artist and made new friends that are on the same wavelength as her.

When it comes to eliminating negative people from your life, you don't want to do so on bad terms. Having enemies is never a good idea so here are a few strategies to assist you in getting rid of the negative Nancy's in your life.

Create Boundaries and Maintain Them: There are some people, like family members and work colleagues, that you can't totally eliminate from your life. So, the most effective way of dealing with such people is to create boundaries and maintain them. In other words, feed them with a long-handled spoon. The first thing you need to do is decide what you will tolerate in a relationship and what you won't. By the way, this is not only something you should do with people you currently know now, but also with new people you meet. When you start to feel that something is not right in your interactions with people, enforce your boundaries and don't back down.

For example, if you have a friend who is always calling you to complain about something, tell him or her that you would appreciate when they call you that they either have something good to say or they don't bother calling you at all. Once that friend realizes that you are serious, and they are not willing to change, they will simply stop calling you because they won't have anything to call you about.

Don't Allow Yourself to be Manipulated: Toxic people always have some emergency crisis that they need you to assist them with. They will call you screaming and crying that you need to come around urgently, and when you get there you find out that it's something as miniscule as they've broken a fingernail! We've all heard the story of the boy who cried wolf, but there may be that one time when there really is an emergency. So, before you leave your house, make sure the issue isn't something you can resolve over the phone instead of wasting your time and just dashing over there.

Understand Projection: Eliminating negative people from your life is a process, and a part of that process involves limiting the amount of power they have over your emotions, and that means understanding that when they are hurting you, they are not really seeing you. What they are actually doing is projecting the parts about themselves that they don't like onto you, and this is usually done via a verbal attack. Their vicious behavior has nothing to do with you, but everything to do with how much they hate themselves.

Don't Give Up: When your negative friends realize that you are no longer falling for their games and are trying to distance yourself, their behavior will get a lot worse. It can become so intense that some people fold and give in to their demands. You have to be relentless. Remind yourself that this is for your benefit and theirs; hopefully, you pulling away might force them to take a good look in the mirror and change their behavior. Either way, once they realize that you are no longer willing to tolerate their antics, they will find another victim to attack.

Get Some New Friends: You are probably going to feel pretty lonely once you have gotten rid of your negative friends; not to worry, you can make new ones. Make a conscious effort to go out to different places. If you don't already have one, start a hobby, or take up a sport or a craft. Be friendly, walk around with a smile on your face, and become the type of person you want to attract.

CHAPTER 9:

DECLUTTERING YOUR THOUGHTS – GETTING YOUR MIND OUT OF THE GUTTER

When you go to sleep at night do you nod off peacefully, or do you lay your head on the pillow with a mind full of chaos and confusion? Most people will agree with the latter. Not only are our homes full of clutter, but our minds are also full of clutter; the average brain is in constant overdrive, thinking, worrying, and being anxious about upcoming events. There is actually nothing wrong with thinking as long as your thoughts are positive and helpful; unfortunately, that is not the case for most of us.

The universe is made up of laws, and there is nothing we can do to change them. If we choose to live by them, they will work for us; if not, they will work against us. The reality is that your current life situation, whether good or bad, is due to the way you think. Your reality is created by your state of mind. Think about it like this, before anything manifests in the physical world, it starts as a thought. The lightbulb was invented by Thomas Edison before the bulb became a reality; he sat down and thought about what it would be like to have a light that you could turn off and on instead of lighting a candle. He then thought about how he could make this device, and then he went on to make it. The light bulb and every other creation in the world started with a thought. If you want to organize your life, the first thing you need to take control of is your thought life. As your thinking pattern is transformed from negative to positive, you will begin to experience a healthy shift in your current reality.

Society teaches us that our feelings are defined by our circumstances when the truth is that our feelings are defined by our thoughts. Every area of your life, from your finances to your health and relationships, are a direct result of your thoughts and your overall belief system. Since we cannot change this reality, the only thing we can do is accept it and make the decision to take dominion over our thoughts instead of them having control over us. Only then will you be able to transform your life and attract the things that you want.

There are no constraints on your thought life, no one can dictate to you how you should think; you are in the driver's seat. Nobody else has access to your mind apart from you; in fact, it is the most powerful possession you own, and once you tap into this reality, you will become unstoppable.

Science continues to confirm that everything in the universe, including our thoughts, is made up of energy. This means that your thoughts are alive, and each time you think about something, depending on what you are thinking about, that energy is either positive or negative.

This book is not about the law of attraction; however, I feel that it is important to mention it here to give you a better understanding of how your thoughts are affecting your life. The main premise of the law of attraction is that energy is like a magnet, it attracts other energy. So, if your thoughts are energy, you attract what you think. There is a value attached to each thought; however, this is something that you determine. The more you think about something, the more powerful that thought becomes and the faster you will see it turn into a reality. The random thoughts you think are not as powerful as your consistent thoughts. However, it is important to mention that if you spend one hour a day thinking positive, but 23 hours a day thinking negative, it is your negative thoughts that will hold the most power. Negative thinking overshadows positive thinking, and positive thinking overshadows negative thinking. Therefore, you create your reality according to what you think about the most.

The mind is made up of two compartments, the conscious and the subconscious mind. The majority of people are unaware of the subconscious mind and how powerful it is. You can compare the subconscious mind to a gigantic warehouse that stores every experience you have ever encountered in life. According to experts, by the age of 21, the subconscious mind has already stored the equivalent of the contents of 100 Encyclopedia Britannica's! During hypnosis, older people are capable of remembering with complete accuracy, things that took place in their life 50 years previously. The subconscious mind is in perfect condition, the problem is the conscious mind.

The subconscious mind is designed to store and retrieve information. Its job is to ensure that your behavior is in alignment with the way you have been programmed. Your words and actions fit a pattern shaped out of the self-concept created by your subconscious mind. There is nothing that the subconscious mind does independently; the only thing it does is obey the orders given to it by the conscious mind. Think about it like this, the job of a gardener is to plant seeds in fertile soil; well, your subconscious mind is the fertile soil, it is made up of the perfect conditions for seeds to take root and grow. So, if your mind plays the role of a gardener and plants seeds of thought into your subconscious mind, it means that whether the thoughts are positive or negative, they are going to grow, and it is these thoughts that are the driving force behind your life.

Your subconscious mind doesn't have a voice. It does not have the ability to tell your conscious mind to stop sending it thoughts, so the seeds that are sown will either become beautiful flowers that will guide you to live your best life or ugly weeds that will ensure all your worst nightmares come true. You are the only person who can choose which seeds are planted.

Those who were brought up in an abusive household hold a memory bank of everything that took place during those years. If you have never been able to understand why there are some people who walk out of one abusive relationship right into another—this is why. The only reality that their subconscious mind knows is abuse; therefore, abuse has become their physical reality and that is what they attract. Even though they know that it is wrong for them to be treated the way they are, and they have a deep desire to get as far away from an abusive partner as possible, they are continuously drawn back because that is what they attract. If they don't get professional help, most people give up and end up believing that is what they deserve in life, and oftentimes, they pass it onto their children. The cycle of abuse then continues until someone gets fed up and puts an end to it.

This all sounds really gloomy, doesn't it? No, it's not a position that anyone wants to be in; but the good news is that there is a way out. You can declutter your mind and live the life that you deserve.

CHAPTER 10:

DECLUTTERING YOUR THOUGHTS – THE POWER OF POSITIVE THINKING

To declutter your mind, you will need to learn to change the way you think. This is not an easy task, but neither is it impossible. From my own personal experience, I can tell you that focusing on the positive instead of the negative will bring much good into your life. However, before I dive into that, what do you think happy and successful people spend their time thinking about? This answer is pretty simple really. They think about the goals they have set for themselves and how they intend to accomplish them. These thoughts shield their minds from negative thinking and help them to develop a positive attitude that propels them into success. On the flip side of things, negative people spend their time thinking and talking about what they don't have and what they don't want in life, which makes them feel miserable and depressed.

How to Develop a Positive Mindset

According to research, positive people are very optimistic. Even in difficult times, they are able to change their perspective and see the light at the end of the tunnel. I refer to these people as eagles. You see, an eagle is one of the strongest birds in nature. When a storm is brewing, all the other birds fly off and hide. However, the eagle loves storms; in fact, they wait in anticipation for them. Eagles like to fly high, and the force of a storm allows them to do so. When the storm arrives, they tilt their body in a certain angle and allow the winds to take them higher. This is what positive people do. They see the storms or problems in their lives different from everyone else, and that's because they look at them from a different angle. They see them as opportunities and use them to push them into something greater. This is not the case with negative people; like the other birds, they run and hide from their problems and see them as the end instead of the beginning. Being positive is all about one thing, and that is state of mind.

The good news about optimism is that it is a quality that you can learn. If you say and do what positive people do, you will become like them. Optimists look for the treasure in every dark place. Instead of getting angry and depressed, they get their emotions in check and say, "What lessons can I learn from what has taken place?" They don't have sleepless nights worrying about their situation; they find solutions and get to work so that they can resolve their problems.

HOW TO TRAIN YOUR BRAIN TO THINK POSITIVE

Training the brain is a simple concept; it is putting it into practice and making it a habit that is difficult. Do you remember what you learned about the subconscious mind? Well, when you decide that you are going to do something that your subconscious mind does not recognize, it will do everything it can to pull you back into your old habits. This is the reason why bad habits are so difficult to break—you are literally fighting against yourself and it doesn't feel very good. The subconscious mind wants to keep you in your comfort zone, and if you are used to thinking negative all the time, thinking positive is stepping outside of your comfort zone. The trick is to push through, and if you mess up, keep going. They say it takes 60 days to develop a habit, so keep working at it and you will eventually get there.

Despite the fact that the mind is an incredibly powerful tool, it only has the capacity to focus on one thought at a time; therefore, your goal is to keep on thinking positive thoughts until new neural pathways are created in the brain. Remember, when something negative happens, the way you respond to it will determine the outcome. That's why it is essential to always look for the positive in any negative situation.

THE POWER OF POSITIVE AFFIRMATIONS

Affirmations are either the words that you say or the thoughts that you think. If you are reading this, there is a high chance you have a habit of saying and thinking not very nice things, which means that your mind is basically full of junk. Positive affirmations open the door to transformation. Let me ask you a question: who is the person you speak to the most? Most people are going to say their boyfriend, girlfriend, or best friend. The truth is that the person you speak to the majority of the time is yourself. We all have an internal dialog, and we are either saying nice things to ourselves or not very nice things. There are several health benefits associated with positive affirmations:

It Eliminates Depression: There are several reasons people suffer from depression; but some of them are low self-esteem, not feeling worthy, and not feeling good enough. Research has found that repeating positive affirmations can help to reverse depression. A study conducted by the University of Arizona found that positive affirmations were an effective supplemental treatment for patients suffering from depression and anxiety. For some of the patients, positive affirmations were more helpful than drugs or therapy.

HOW TO USE POSITIVE AFFIRMATIONS

There are three ways that you can use positive affirmations. For them to be the most effective, I would strongly advise that you use all three.

1. **Thought Replacement:** The majority of the time we don't even realize what we are thinking about. According to experts, we think between 12,000-70,000 thoughts per day! That's a lot of thoughts; however, these are automatic thoughts that we will never remember. If I told you to write

down your last 1,000 thoughts, you would look at me like I was crazy. These are not the thoughts you need to be concerned about, because they are not the thoughts you focus on. The trick is that you need to catch yourself when you are thinking negative thoughts and replace them with a positive affirmation.

2. **Affirmation Repetition:** This involves setting aside a time each day and standing in front of a mirror and repeating affirmations.

3. **Affirmation Meditation:** No, I am not talking about the type of meditation that involves sitting with your legs crossed and chanting. You can also meditate by repeating words continuously. This is also referred to as murmuring. The aim of affirmation meditation is to get you into the habit of thinking positive so that there is no room in your mind to think negative thoughts. The aim is to spend the entire day silently saying affirmations under your breath. If there is no one around, you can say them out loud.

HERE ARE 25 POSITIVE AFFIRMATIONS TO GET YOU OUT OF THE HABIT OF NEGATIVE THINKING.

1. I will live the life of my dreams.
2. I possess the tools I need to succeed in life.
3. I am stronger than my struggles.

4. I am in control of my life.

5. I am fierce.

6. I have the power to motivate myself.

7. I will achieve every goal I have set for myself.

8. I am not afraid of the fire because I am the fire.

9. I deserve the best out of life and nothing less.

10. I have the choice to decide who I become in life.

11. I am allowed to say "no" sometimes.

12. Happiness is a reality for me.

13. I speak with self-assurance and confidence.

14. There are no limits to my confidence.

15. I am worthy to be loved unconditionally.

16. I choose to be hopeful instead of fearful.

17. I choose to be positive instead of negative.

18. I will not allow other people's negative emotions to affect me.

19. I am committed to becoming the best version of myself.

20. I am not defined by my circumstances.

21. I am bold and beautiful.

22. I love myself unconditionally.

23. I am responsible for creating the life that I want.

24. I will only think thoughts of peace, love, and harmony.

25. I will not waste my energy on negative self-talk.

CHAPTER 11:

DECLUTTERING YOUR DAY – ENHANCING YOUR TIME MANAGEMENT SKILLS

D o you feel as if there are not enough hours in the day to get things done? If you answered yes to this question, it's probably because you spend too much time doing fruitless activities that you don't get time to do what really needs to be done. According to statistics, the average American household spends 7 hours and 50 minutes watching TV per day. So, people are not spending their time doing constructive and beneficial activities that will enhance their lives, like reading, studying or exercising; they are slumped in front of a TV! To compound the issue, we are now living in an era where social media has taken over the world. Research suggests that the average person spends around two hours per day on social media! So, if there are only 24 hours in a day and eight of those are spent asleep, that means we are awake for 16 hours per day. And fourteen of them per week are spent with our eyes glued to a screen! Not to mention all the other things we are doing in between. Can you see why you never get anything done?

One of the main differences between the successful and the unsuccessful people in the world is that they know how to manage their time, and they are extremely particular about it. Let's take a look at some of their daily routines.

Sir Richard Branson is the founder of the Virgin Group conglomerate, and he has a net worth of $5 billion. In a 2014 blog post, Branson documented his daily routine, which included:

- Waking up at 5:00 am
- Breakfast with his family
- Responding to emails
- Yoga and Tai Chi
- Carrying a notebook to write down inspiration throughout the day
- Rarely watches TV
- Dinner with family
- In bed by 11:00 pm

Bill Gates is the founder of Microsoft and is known as one of the wealthiest men in the world. According to Forbes, he has an estimated net worth of $96.5 billion.

- Wakes up at 4:30 am
- Works out on the treadmill at the same time as watching teaching DVDs
- Reads the newspaper

- He breaks up his schedule into five-minute intervals
- He keeps track of his exceptionally busy day by note taking
- Spends time reading
- When he is not working, he enjoys spending time with his three children
- He enjoys playing bridge on the weekends
- He washes the dishes every night

Elon Musk is the CEO and founder of Neuralink and Tesla; he has a net worth of $19.8 billion.

- Wakes up at 7:00 AM
- Checks and responds to emails
- Interacts with his sons and sends them to school
- Takes a shower and makes his way to work
- He refuses to waste time on anything that doesn't make things better
- In his free time, he enjoys hanging out with friends, watching movies, and playing games with his children

Warren Buffet is the most successful investor in the world; he has an estimated net worth of $77.7 billion.

- He wakes up at 6:45 AM
- Reads *Forbes, USA Today*, and the *Wall Street Journal*
- Has breakfast
- Does some exercise

- Goes to work and spends 80% of his day reading
- Unwinds after work by playing bridge
- Goes to bed at 10:45 PM

Okay, so we have looked at the daily routines of some of the most successful people in the world, and one thing they have in common is that they all use their time very productively. Did you notice that there was no mention of watching TV? These people are billionaires and run multi-billion-dollar corporations, yet they still find time for leisure activities and spending time with their families.

If you want to get more done during the day and achieve the goals that you have set for yourself, you are going to need to completely rearrange your life and do some careful planning. Most people will admit that their daily routine looks something like this:

- Set the alarm for 7:00 am but hit the snooze button until 7:30 am
- Jump out of bed and take a shower
- Get the kids ready (if you have them)
- Rush out the door
- Grab breakfast on the go
- Work for 8 hours
- Come home
- Have dinner
- Sit in front of the TV
- Go to bed
- Repeat until the weekend

Here are a few tips to assist you in managing your time better so that you can be more productive throughout the day.

Create a Daily Routine: We all know how important it is for children to have a daily routine to give them some discipline and structure. I am sure you can remember being told what time to go to bed, wake up, have dinner, do your homework, etc. when you were younger. But as you grew older, this routine became less and less important until you collapsed into a very unorganized life schedule with no boundaries. I am sure you can admit this. The majority of adults don't have a set routine and just go through their day without a plan and hope for the best. The way a child feels stressed and anxious when they have no routine is the same way adults feel stressed and anxious when they have no routine, but they just don't realize that something so simple is the main cause of their frustration in life.

Many people share the view that routines are boring, stifling, and rigid; but as you have learned from the lives of highly successful people, a strict daily routine is actually the path to productivity, freedom, happiness, and becoming the best version of ourselves. Here are a few benefits associated with having a daily routine.

Creates Structure: A daily routine gives us the much-needed structure and logical sequence required to live our lives and go about our daily affairs. After some time, this routine becomes a habit and we become comfortable and familiar with what we have to do each day.

Establishes Good Habits: Repetition is the secret to building good habits. When we create a personal routine, it helps us develop good habits as we repeat the same tasks each day. Think about it like this: at a minimum, the majority of people brush their teeth first thing in the morning—it's automatic, you don't even think about it, you just do it. Once your daily routine becomes a habit, it too will become automatic.

Break Bad Habits: A daily routine will not only help you build good habits, but it will also help you break bad habits because your good habits will slowly start to replace the bad ones.

Get Our Priorities in Order: There are certain things in your life that are more important than others; however, much of the time they don't get done because other non-essential activities take their place. When you have a routine in place, you know exactly what you need to do on any given day.

Eliminates Procrastination: When routine becomes habit, as mentioned, we just do things automatically. So we are basically doing things subconsciously, which eliminates procrastination and enables us to quickly do the things we need to do without continuously putting them off to the following day.

Builds Momentum: Momentum is very important when it comes to achieving goals. When you think about the end result, getting there seems impossible; however, if you are doing something small each day to get to your final destination, you are more likely to get there.

Builds Self Confidence: When you are unable to achieve your goals or you are constantly leaving projects undone, it is soul destroying. There is no one to blame other than yourself, and this is not something you want to make a habit out of. However, when you have a strict routine in place and you are constantly working towards your goals, confidence is built as you achieve them.

Wake Up Early: We have all heard the saying, "The early bird gets the worm," and as you read, all of the successful people mentioned waking up before 7:00 AM. There are several benefits to waking up early.

- **Time to Yourself:** This is especially true if you have children. In the early hours of the morning when no one is awake, there are no cars outside, no noise, just you and your thoughts. It's a good time to think and reflect and decide how you are best going to tackle your day. It allows you to prepare yourself to start your routine instead of jumping out of bed and springing into action because you don't have the time.

- **Increased Productivity:** Since everyone else is asleep, waking up early allows you to get things done while there are no distractions. For example, if one of your goals is to write a book, you can use this time to write a few pages. Writing a book is a huge task; however, a journey of a thousand miles starts with a single step. Even if you write one page a day, you can write a book within a year.

- **Makes You Feel More Positive:** A sense of achievement is a great feeling, and you are more likely to experience this when you wake up early. You see, extra time means that you can get more things done, like having breakfast, exercising, or working on a project. You will no longer feel the same pressure and stress of when you wake up late and have to rush around trying to get things done.

- **Peak Will Power:** Studies have shown that will power is at its peak first thing in the morning. The best time to work on your goals is after you've had a good night's sleep and your energy has been renewed. As you go throughout the day, your energy and will power is depleted, and so when you return home after a hard day's work you are less likely to do the things you had planned.

- **Peaceful Commute:** Whether you drive to work or get public transport everyone can relate to the stress of rush hour traffic. The good news is that when you wake up early and leave the house early, you avoid this. It allows you to get to work before everyone else and get ahead of your deadlines.

To-do Lists

Do you constantly feel overwhelmed because of all the things that you need to get done? Do you forget to do certain things? Or miss deadlines? If you have answered yes to any of these questions, then a to-do list will help you organize and prioritize your tasks.

By writing a list of things that you need to do, you ensure that everything you need to accomplish is written down in front of you so that you don't leave anything out. And by listing the activities in order of importance, you can prioritize which of them you are going to do first. To-do lists are crucial if you are going to overcome work overload. However, there is more to it than simply writing out a list, you must learn to use them effectively. Here are some tips to help you.

Step 1: Make a list of all the tasks you need to get out of the way. If you have a lot of different things to get done, you might find it easier to write several lists, for example, work, study, home.

Step 2: Put a letter or a number next to each task to list them in order of priority and then write the list out again in order.

Step 3: Work your way through the list in order and as you complete each task, tick them off the list.

To-do List Software: Using paper is a great way to get started writing to-do lists but you can be much more efficient using software. You will need to take some time out to teach yourself how to use the software, but once you've mastered it, you'll find the program very easy to use. One of the main benefits of using software is that it reminds you of things you need to get done urgently, and you can synchronize it with your email and phone so that you always have your list at hand. A Google search will pull up a list of recommended software.

Goal Setting: When was the last time you set a goal for yourself and actually achieved it? The sad truth is that the average person doesn't set goals, they simply coast through life, and then when they reach 50 wonder why they haven't achieved anything significant. As you have probably realized by now, time waits for no man, and so the most essential element of time is what you choose to do with it. Therefore, setting goals for yourself and timeframes in which to accomplish them is one of the most productive things you can do.

When deciding what to do with your time, your main focus should be on your goals and how everything you do is aimed at bringing you a little bit closer to achieving those goals.

WHY SET GOALS?

Entrepreneurs, athletes, and high achievers in any career all set goals for themselves. Goal setting provides you with something to focus on for the long term and motivation to achieve for the short term. They allow you to use the knowledge that you have already gained to assist you in making the most out of your life. By setting goals that are concise and clear, you can keep track of your progress and feel good about yourself once you have achieved them. When you get the dream out of your head and put it down on paper, it turns a seemingly impossible task into something realistic.

WHERE DO I START?

Now that you have decided on what goals you want to achieve, it is important that you make a plan to achieve them. Think about it this way, if you are about to drive to a destination you are not familiar with, do you use a GPS to get you to your location or waste time driving around all over town trying to find it? Well, the same principle applies in life—you can either drift around aimlessly without any direction or focus, or you can make a plan.

Goal setting is a powerful process that allows you to think about the best future for yourself, which then provides the motivation to push you towards achieving your goals. Goal setting helps you decide what direction you want to take in life. When you know where you want to go, you know where to keep your focus, and you stop wasting time on fruitless activities that distract you from doing what needs to be done to accomplish your goals.

When it comes to writing down your goals don't be shy, there is nothing wrong with dreaming big. After all, where would we be in the world today if people didn't dream big? Things like the laptop I am using to type this book would never have been invented. So, that gigantic mansion you can see yourself living in, write it down. The word "dream" is often misused; the assumption is that because something can't be seen with the natural eye it can't be a reality. For example, if you tell someone that you have a dream of owning your own business one day when you are working in a factory on minimum wage, that person will most likely look at you as if you have lost your mind because you don't have the required credentials. Your dream is specific to you; it belongs to you, and you have the ability to turn it into a reality—don't let anyone tell you otherwise.

When you write your end goal down on paper, it is going to look intimidating. Your first thought is going to be, "Well, how am I ever going to achieve something like this?" Not to worry, there is a strategy, and if you follow it, success is inevitable.

When you set lifetime goals, it clarifies your perspective and becomes the driving force behind the decisions that you make. If you are not sure about the goals you should be setting for yourself, here are a few ideas.

Career: What level do you want to get to in your career? Do you want to become a partner, a CEO, a manager?

Financial: How much money do you want to earn? If you are in a career that won't give you this opportunity, you will need to switch careers.

Education: To achieve your career goals, are there certain qualifications you will need to acquire? For example, if you want to become an accountant, what certifications would you need to get?

Family: Do you have a desire to get married by a certain age? Would you like to have children? If so, how many? Do you have an ideal partner in mind?

Attitude: Are there things about your character that you would like to change? Do you get angry easily? Are you easily offended?

Physical: Do you consider yourself to be overweight? Do you have an ideal body type that you would wish to achieve?

Public Service: Are there things you would like to do in the community? Are there people you would like to help?

Spend some time brainstorming some ideas. There is no need to go overboard, you don't want to choose goals in every category and overwhelm yourself. It is advised that you have no more than 10 significant goals.

Goal Breakdown

Once you have determined what your lifetime goals are, write out a five-year plan that details the smaller goals you will need to accomplish to achieve the larger ones.

Your next step should be to write out a list of daily goals you will need to achieve to turn your ultimate goal into a reality. For example, if you need to gain qualifications for career goals, your short-term goals should be a daily study plan to ensure you have the knowledge to pass your exams. The idea is to take micro steps towards your goals instead of trying to rush them when you realize the deadline is fast approaching.

Stay on Track

Don't work blindly—pay attention to what you are doing at all times. A good way to do this is to set yourself weekly reminders to check how far you have progressed. If you are not where you need to be, you will need to figure out why and come up with another strategy.

S.M.A.R.T Goals

A great way to get the most out of the goal-setting process is to use the SMART technique. SMART stands for: Specific, Measurable, Attainable, Relevant and Timely. There are several versions of this type of goal setting, but in general, the SMART method helps you get more specific about your goals. For example, you wouldn't just write, "I want to become a lawyer." You would write, "I want to become a lawyer by December 2020." The idea is that once you put a date on a goal, it prevents you from procrastinating and encourages you to take steps towards the goal.

Bonus Goal Setting Tips

Turn your goals into a positive affirmation: Instead of writing, "I want to get married and have three children by the age of 35." Write, "I am married with three children by the age of 35." When you speak about a goal in the present tense, the subconscious mind records the information as if it has already taken place. This process makes manifestation easier.

Be Specific: If you are not sure about what you want, achieving it is going to be difficult. Make sure that you are extremely specific about what you want down to very last detail. Include information such as dates, times, and amounts.

Set Priorities: Some of your goals are going to be more important to you than others; therefore, list your goals in order of priority and work on them in that order.

Be Realistic: I encourage everyone I know to dream big; however, it is also important that you are realistic, or you will set yourself up for failure. For example, having a goal that you will lose 20 lbs. in one week is not a good idea.

Don't stop once you have achieved your goals—life should never become stagnant. Always have something to focus on, that motivates you, and pushes you forward. In fact, one of your most important goals should be continuous self-improvement.

STOP PROCRASTINATING

One of the most dangerous dream killers is procrastination—time waits for no man, and it isn't going to wait for you. Procrastination is delaying things that you could do today until the following day. Before you know it, ten years have passed without you achieving your goal!

Procrastination is often taken as a joke, or spoken of lightly, when in reality it is an extremely destructive force that has the power to stop you from moving forward in life. If procrastination is something you want to eradicate from your life, this chapter will help you to do so.

Recognizing Procrastination: The majority of people know full well when they are procrastinating. It's not difficult to work out that you have a deadline in an hour, but you are emailing your boyfriend about your upcoming romantic getaway! Here are some of the main symptoms of procrastination.

- You have several things to do within the day but none of them are important
- Getting ready to complete something and then deciding that you need a cup of coffee or a sandwich
- Leaving the most important jobs on your to-do list until last
- Waiting until you feel like doing something before getting on with it

It's also important to mention what procrastination isn't— leaving insignificant tasks until a later date. There will be times when there are some things that have to be put on hold because something else is more important. For example, you may have a deadline, but you also have a doctor's appointment that you have to attend. There are also going to be times when you simply don't have the energy to do certain tasks. If you are tired, sleep—it's important that you listen to your body so you don't end up doing a bad job, or worse, get sick from overworking yourself.

WHY DO YOU PROCRASTINATE?

There are many different reasons people procrastinate. If the task is something that you don't enjoy doing, you are going to put it off for as long as you can. All jobs are going to have things about them that we don't like. The key is to get them done so that we can put our energy into the aspects of the job that we like.

In general, disorganized people don't have a specific system in place when it comes to doing certain things. So they just do things with their eyes closed and hope for the best. Organized people, on the other hand, create to-do lists and schedules that have been prioritized. They take note of when the task must be completed, the importance attached to each task, and the length of time it will take to complete the task. Organized people are also good at just getting things done. They stay away from procrastination and they don't like being unproductive. They make life easier for themselves by breaking each activity down into manageable chunks so that the project doesn't overwhelm them.

Some people are intimidated by certain tasks because they know that they don't have the skills required to get it done, and therefore, focus on things that they know they can complete so they don't have to deal with feeling inadequate. Then there are some people who are afraid of success—they don't like failure either—but success scares them even more. Any amount of success is going to be life changing because it brings on additional responsibility, and there are some people who don't want to deal with that.

STRATEGIES TO PREVENT PROCRASTINATION

Procrastination is a habit—it isn't something that you developed overnight, so don't expect it to disappear overnight. You are going to have to put some work in if you want to overcome it. A habit is no longer a habit once you have stopped participating in it. You are more likely to eradicate procrastination from your life if you implement as many of these strategies as possible. Go through each one and decide what works best for you.

Consequences: Focus your mind on what will happen if you miss the deadline. Is there a possibility that you might get a disciplinary warning? Could you lose pay? If you are self-employed will it mean a bad review?

Reward Yourself: Rewarding yourself is a great incentive to get things done. It doesn't need to be anything big, whether it's a new pair of shoes, a movie, or a bar of chocolate, establish a system of reward that's going to motivate you to get things completed.

Accountability Partner: Having someone to report to is a bit like peer pressure. Most people don't want to look like a fool in front of their friends, so they will do what needs to be done to impress them. Diet clubs and self-help groups swear by this method because it works so well.

Get Organized: This is a no brainer really, but it's worth mentioning to remind you of how important it really is. Organization is the key to success. Here are a few tips you can implement to become more organized and avoid procrastination.

1. **Plan Your Projects:** Create a schedule for each day that details the process you are going to take for completing each task and how long it will take for you to get them done.

2. **To do Lists:** This is another reminder, but it's important—to do lists help you to stay on top of things. When you attempt to remember what you need to do, you are bound to forget.

3. **Set Goals:** In general, you will know how long it is going to take to complete each task. A great way to motivate yourself is to set time goals to finish each task within a certain amount of time.

4. **Don't Multitask:** No matter how many deadlines you've got, never try to do all of them at once. Focus on one task at a time.

So now you know all about procrastination and how to avoid it, that's great. Knowledge is power, but implementation is even more powerful!

CONCLUSION

I have no idea what it is that you want out of life, but what I do know is that you picked up this book because you want things in your life to change. May I submit to you that before you become a public success, you must first become a success in private. What you do behind closed doors is more important than what you do in front of a crowd because what you do in secret is what truly defines your character. Private preparation is how you get ready to go to the next level in your life.

When I started my personal journey to decluttering my life, I had no idea that it would lead me to what I am doing today. Cleaning up and cleaning out placed my feet on the road to success. When my environment was transformed, my mindset was transformed. As my home was renovated, my heart was renovated. Orderliness in my home brought orderliness to my life and that is what propelled me into my purpose in life.

Decluttering my home and getting organized had more to do with getting prepared for my destiny than my house looking like a show home. It's one thing to take the time out to reconstruct your home, but maintenance is an entirely different level of discipline. There are some people who spend every January getting their house in order, but by the end of February, it's a mess again. There is nothing easy about this task by any means. In fact, it's extremely difficult, and there are going to be days when you simply can't be bothered. However, if you don't want to be average, you can't live like the average person. And this relates to every area of your life, not just your home.

It's up to you to put the demands on your life to improve and grow. Seek after excellence and success will seek after you.

I wish you all the best in your pursuit of living a minimal, decluttered, and organized life!

THANKS FOR READING!

I really hope you enjoyed this book, and most of all got more value from it than you had to give.

It would mean a lot to me if you left an Amazon review – I will reply to all questions asked!

Simply find this book on Amazon, scroll to the reviews section, and click "Write a customer review".

Or alternatively please visit www.pristinepublish.com/minimalismreview to leave a review.

Be sure to check out my email list, where I am constantly adding tons of value. The best way to currently get on the list is by visiting www.pristinepublish.com/meditationbonus and entering your email.

Here I'll provide actionable information that aims to improve your enjoyment of life. I'll update you on my latest books, and I'll even send free e-books that I think you'll find useful.

Kindest regards,

Also by

Olivia Telford

With Hygge and Mindfulness you'll discover something that offers relaxation, happiness, and contentment, all rolled into one. They encompass the positivity and enjoyment that one can get from simple everyday things.

Visit: www.pristinepublish.com/olivia

Printed in Great Britain
by Amazon